The Power to Connect

Charles J Shovlin

ORIGINAL WRITING

978-1-907179-06-8

A CIP catalogue for this book is available from the National Library.

Published by Original Writing Ltd., Dublin, 2009.

Printed by Cahills, Dublin.

Contents

Dedications

I dedicate this book to all the great thinkers and teachers in the new millennium

Introduction

On the 25th of May 2006 I open my PC on a blank page and wrote down the words "the power to connect", having no reason why I did that and no sooner had I these words down in writing than, I sense strong vibrations around me and intuitively I hear the words **Greetings my friend.** It has certainly been a while since I had messages of this nature. Yes ten years to the day I channelled my first messages in the book " A way To Healing The Seven Set Practice", which some of you would have read by now. Yes my spiritual guide from his time 1500 BC has made contact with me once again, to channel more messages in this book "The Power To Connect". Since the last contact in the book "A Way To Healing The Seven Set Practice" the vibrations have shifted and not alone that but I am happy to say that the vibrations of the whole planet earth have shifted as well. This of course makes my writing much easier this time round. Although this writing does not seem as fast as Automatic writing, it is still perhaps Automatic writing but much slower. However, it is not that I have slowed down as I had first thought; my spiritual guide assures me; that as a channel I am working now on the seventh vibration which leaves it much easier for me to pick up these messages. However that said; I am still operating within the dense energies of the earth between fourth and fifth vibrations, which sometimes make things confusing, but most of the time it's fine.

So the messages in this book do not seem as mixed up as the early stages of my last book " A Way To Healing The Seven Set Practice " and indeed not as tiring. I seem to have no problem in writing them down on my PC. So yes I would say that the vibrations have definitely shifted since then., just look around you.

However, to make this book more accessible to the reader I have used the word **you / lightworkers** right throughout these messages.

Read the book as if you were listing to a wise higher intelligent being, which you are, or you can visualise yourself going somewhere in your mind and receiving these messages from a wise highly intelligent being. You can call this wise highly intelligent being; your guardian angel, higher-self, or your spirit guide the choice is yours. Enjoy the book and the messages within it. I hope by reading this book that it will expand your mind and reconnect you to a higher intelligence of collective consciousness within yourself; i.e. your soul

Remember what you choose to believe or what you choose not to believe within these writings for whatever reason; is not important, but what is important is that you connect to the true spirit within.

Messages

Although since our last encounter I was never too far away from you or your vibrations. I could not interfere with your journey because of the law of free will, which thankfully people on your planet are beginning to understand and respect a lot more since my last contact. May I first start by congratulating you on your journey so far? I know it hasn't been easy for you. This was because of the dense vibration of your planet but as you can see consciousness is shifting and now that you and many like you (lightworkers) have shifted into the fifth dimension or vibration I think vibration is a better name for it, the journey will be much easier. Indeed now that you have come to trust the universe and trust the process of life and your understanding of its laws, you will be able to shift consciousness ever further on the planet.

I have called it your planet earth but as you know by now with your shift in awareness, (and may I congratulate you again on this) that you and many of your kind (lightworkers) come from many worlds Arcturus, Sirius and Pleiades just to mention a few. Indeed you were enjoying paradise like communities complete with the array of colour splendour and wonder with castle, Crystal gardens and waterfalls. You were asked by a committee of guides like myself from the Chamber of Council to come to earth to help in further evolution of the planet. And you reluctantly agreed to return to earth. This is why you felt your body weak and didn't want to make any connection with the earth in the beginning and you even got angry at times.

Indeed many of your kind did not stay here due to the heavy density of the shifting energy. Others relegated themselves to an earth life, but again felt depressed or angry about it. The ones that fared out the best, were like yourselves who study some form of spirituality such as kabbilistic, Wicca, Astrology, paganism rituals, crystal healing, hierology, candle invocation, Taiji, shamanism and the likes.

So many of you are from other worlds that had many incarnations on earth down through the ages. As you also know that this is possibly many of you're i.e. (lightworkers) last incarnation and again may myself as high priest from the planet Arcturus of the Chamber of Counsel of love and light thank you i.e. (lightworkers) for your voluntary work on planet earth.

As high priest from the planet Arcturus of love and light or what you on earth would call the legendary civilisations of Atlantis and Lemuria more on this later (see chamber of science). My work is with the Chamber of Council, I can only give you an idea of how this planet operates as even at your stage of human consciousness, which would be regarded primitive to us as you would perhaps regard the Stone Age as primitive to you now. This in mind I can only give you an idea how this planet operates in the seventh vibration / seven vibrations, which everyone on earth's evolution eventually can reach. Please excuse me if I repeatedly emphasise this statement through out this book. It is a most profound statement indeed and should be given a lot of attention within homes, churches and states.

Well to give you a scale on things very roughly and then I will go into things in more detail as this book develops.

As you know the earth is part of the Milky Way galaxy with a population of 6.5 billion souls. Well Arcturus belongs to the galaxy of Saturn, not the planet Saturn but a galaxy beyond it with a population of 62.7 billion souls. We have no "sunlight" as such, everywhere is brightened by subdued light that makes earth extremely dull, dreary and lifeless by comparison to Arcturus.

We have no wars, no cars, no killing either people or animal, it would be unheard of as animals communicated with people on a much higher level than that on Earth. Dolphins are the nearest example I can give you in human evolution at present. Dolphins carry a great deal of light but sadly they are moving off the planet, however elephants, whales and the feline kingdom will be the next great carries of light. These animals are holding the shift in consciousness at present and they will communicate with more and more people as time progress. This practice is second to none on Arcturus as animals and many other creatures communicate telepathically on Arcturus. There is no money. The nearest thing to money in earthly terms is Crystal. Crystal is everywhere and in everything from cloths to furniture to buildings, jewellery from the binding of books to household utensils, everything, and has great healing properties. (See Chamber of Crystal).

The population is made up of both male and female like earth though perhaps a little more eccentric in fashion and design than on earth. However fashion is much the same only there is no one walking around in pin stripes suits carrying brief cases wearing heels, no pollutions, no government, guards, armies, none of that. Everyone here is more relaxed and in their correct place, according to their vibration, thoughts and personalities.

You may ask how a planet of 62.7 billion souls can be governed without any government. Well the nearest thing we have to a government is a Chamber of Council, which oversees the workings of other Chambers, a bit like N.A.T.O. the United Nations on earth (see Chamber of Council). None get sick here, however if they do get low in energy they are sent to the Chamber of Crystal, which is sort of a healing hospital in earthly terms. Indeed you have one at present in China and many more Qi gong centres through the world. The Center in China was established in 1988 in the city of Zigachong and later, in 1992, relocated to the city of Fengrun, two hours by train from Beijing. It is directed by its founder, Dr. Pang Ming, a Qigong grandmaster and physician trained in both Western and Chinese traditional medicine. This hospital is the largest of its kind in China. Although this place is similar to the Chamber of Crystals it is only the start of a new mind state as none get sick here, in the seventh vibration as there is no death only transition, more on this later (See Chamber of Transformation and Transition).

However people do get low in energy sometimes due to the influx of other souls from other worlds or due to the high interaction of energy at this time on a universal scale. You see now; or should at least becoming to an understanding that everything is governed by energy, money in your world, again it's another form of energy only energy, nothing more nothing less. When people realise this, it will have served it purpose. It is not money that is the root of all-evil but it is the entrapment of money that is the root of all-evil, (more on this later). This was briefly tapped into the book "A way to Healing The Seven Set Practice" The vibrations at that time on the planet were all over the place and many of you weren't strong enough to interact with those vibration, it was only in August 1997 that the shift came into place. Princess Diana was chosen to make this shift as she carried a great deal of light, but please do not make her out to be a saint she would not want you to. There have been others like her, Elvis Presley came about to join the black community with the white community, Marilyn Munroe came about to join the gap between rich and poor and many like Martian Luther King, John Lennon, Mother Teresa and all the saints, St Martha, just to mention a few. These all carry a great deal of light, some more than others but each one equally important in human evolution. They all have awareness of spirit and they have left their mark. Just look around you; their names are still as strong as ever and some names like St Martha go back to the 1st centaury, and people still call her miraculous. However, this is all a question of faith and sadly a gift many on the planet lack today (see Chamber of Connection). However thankfully through more awareness of spirit, quiet time, daily meditation and the likes you (lightworkers) vibrations and the planet vibrations are much higher now. You will come to realise this for yourselves by your own temperament, calmness and connection to higher self and to your shift in consciousness.

Arcturus is made up of much the same minerals as the earth only more crystal like and of course due to the high growth rate in nature, trees, plants and flowers etc, the oxygen level is much higher and the air is not polluted with cars etc, not like on earth, there is no need for them. Everyone can go from one place to another just by thinking they are there, it's that simple. So there is no need for public transport or machines, so no pollutants. This leaves the water's in rivers, lakes and some seas drinkable. There is vegetation everywhere loads of fresh fruit and vegetables, so loads to eat and drink. However, due to the high vibrations the body does not need as much proteins as you do here on earth. The subtle body lives a lot on subdued light energy subdued time or quiet time something like your meditation also known as the Crystallite body. Indeed there are people on the planet earth at present who have made this shift in fact there are 500 at present living on light as they call it or DOW www.selfempowermentacademy.com Divine light within. So with our new hospital in China and people living on light or prana in many parts of the world, maybe this book is not as so far out of reach as it seems when reading the first chapters.

This is why meditation is so important for you/lightworkers and for the people on the planet earth as the change in vibrations comes about.

The houses are built on a control plan order from the Chamber of Science built to suit the individual's mood, personality and vibration, or built to suit the moods, personalities and vibrations of the groups of individuals that share the houses.

There is no family structure of marriage like you have on earth, again look at what's been happening on earth recently on these matters. Souls tend to commune in-group in town and city-like structures, but as I have already said without the transport system as everyone can travel simply by thought. As there is no time band here as in the third dimension, when people think of being somewhere or with someone they are automatically with that space, it's as simple as that. As already said there are both sexes here but as there is no death, there is no birth. However there is transition of souls (see chamber of transformation & transition). I'm glad to see that this word has been brought into the earth's vocabulary. There is no darkness only subdued light, depending on personalities, thoughts and mood swings of the people. The sky is blue and purple red on account of the high level of oxygen in the atmospheres. You may ask, as I know your thoughts because of my level of awareness, what do we do all day long. Well as already stated there is no time so we don't think of a day being long; we just be. However, we don't sit around doing nothing every minute of our day as you put it, it is spent in working for the glory and grace of the Divine. We see everything connected as light and love as unconditional love is the most powerful force in the universe.

I mention that no one wears suits, collars or ties or heels, most people dress according to their moods and personalities, being really true to themselves as no one hides behind masks here like they do on earth. There would be no point because everyone can read everyone's thoughts telepathically, (see telepathy). However in saying that, there is the greatest respect for people's privacy and this is another law of the universe on the inner realms. Everyone communicates telepathically, a skill like many other skills, which indeed is reappearing on earth at present as the shift in consciousness comes about. Indeed this shift is sometimes brought to our awareness by the media through film and books like the "Secret", and the TV series "Heroes" and the likes. In "Heroes" we are led to believe that a majority of people on this planet have extraordinary skills and that they are coming together to save the planet though some choose to use these skill in a negative way. In a way this might be, though with the coming shift of consciousness people are coming together and sharing their gifts, which in the past would be regarded as supernatural, but to most these gifts are natural. So the series the "Heroes" didn't get everything wrong really. It perhaps brings awareness to our own source of power, which is evolving all the time. However in the book / film the "Secret" I think most people are getting the wrong idea especially with the law of attraction, thinking that if they think positively they will get a million euros or the fancy car. I'm afraid it's not quite that simple, this is just wishful thinking and anyway this is not the message. The main message in all of this is thinking positively surely but in a collective conscious way. That is everyone on the planet will have to change his or her old ways of negative thinking, to positively think collectively. To give you a simple example; say someone asked you how you are; don't just say "I am not so bad", but get into the mind set of saying things like "I'm wonderful" and don't wear you heart on your sleeve. Some people may argue the point here that this is like boasting i.e. "sure I'm in great health", "sure I've never been better" and sure as eggs you will be sick the next day, why is that? Well the last example is boasting but the first example is not. In the first example your just saying how you feel. However you may have a pain or some ill and someone asks you "how are you"? By saying to them "I'm wonderful" you're not giving any extra energy to focus on the pain if you say "I don't feel well" or "I have pain and discomforts" etc they might in turn say sure I have this or that wrong with me etc. This will in turn give the negative energy i.e. (thought / pain) more power and everyone continue in bad health and the drama continues. It works the same for boasting about your health, wealth etc. You are loosing power because you are giving away your power. I have heard a lot of old people saying things like when asked "how are they", "thank God I'm not so bad". This is good practice because it holds gratitude; to be grateful is one of the spiritual gifts of the universe. However to say "your not so bad" this holds some doubt on your part and still gives away your power because of the doubt and you will probably continue in the not so well state. You will depend on outside sources for the continuation of good health i.e. your therapist or GP giving them your power or their power over you to make you better instead of connecting to your inner consciousness and getting the strength from within. This is not taking away anything from our therapist or Doctors, as some Doctors are wonderful healers and indeed the word Doctor really means to teach, i.e. to teach you to stay healthy. So if everyone on the planet would shift their mind set a little more positively in a collective respectful manner in all ways, then the sky would certainly be the limit. This is the shift to the seventh vibration.

Back to the Arcturus; the women wear low shoes, sandals made up of much jewellery and the finest soft material. All material has holistic healing qualities in design, colour and fabric. Mostly woman wear their hair long or up in a bun though some chose to have no hair. Some of the more eccentric types wear wigs of all shapes and colours and a few do wear their hair short. Most of the cloths are made from the finest of silk satin and of course with crystal trimmings. Women wear long flowing gowns woven into one, or some wear dresses with pyjama - like bottoms cut short above the knee or ankle. The colour is the most amazing thing about these garments some are designed in the colours of the Chakras (see Chakras). Nearly all women wear a crystal belt, necklace, bracelets or bangles and some wear bracelets on their ankles In fact all jewellery is made up of some crystal, which is manifested in the chamber of science (see chamber of science).

The dresses would be made of layers upon layers, but the eccentric types wear whatever the mood takes them. Clothes are made of a very light material with light vibrations and all clothes have a healing quality about them either in colour, design or fabric. There is no birth so there isn't any sex between souls but there is subdued energy exchange. The nearest example that I can give you in earthly terms is in the film called the "Cocoon" but more powerful and more soul connected than sex on earthly terms.

Men wear clothes similar to the women but with different vibrations i.e. colours & designs. Men wear one piece woven gowns, as do women or two-piece pyjama - like suits with the trousers cut short at the knee again. The trousers are made of layers upon layers from the finest light material. Most men again wear their hair long or with ponytail. Most men wear beards and sandals and some high Priest's carry crystals staffs, they also wear jewellery of crystal belts and medallions and bracelets. But again there are the eccentric types and they dress in many different styles, some men even go so far as to paint their toe nails but here in this world everyone is treated with the utmost reverence and respect and with the greatest love.

There are no outcasts, we have also the chamber of fantasy where you can carry out any fantasies without interfering with the laws of free will. This would be close to virtual reality which will be the next major step in human evolution or technology to explain the fourth and fifth vibrations more on this later.,(see chamber of fantasy).

I said there was no sex but there is a subdued energy exchange and there is the greatest respect for the body. Again the body here is not unlike the earthly body but composed of much lighter vibration. This is the planet of the seventh vibration but when souls reach the fifth vibration they can come here or transcend here.

You have reached the fifth vibration on earth, but you come from the seventh vibration and during healings and meditations you enter the seventh vibration and through that process you are receiving the awareness of spirit of other souls. I'm coming from the chamber of love light and I work with you.

Again this is all explained later; some souls from Angelic, planet or vibrations of the eighth and ninth rays or Ascended masters will come here to Arcturus and bring extra light with them through their being, to help the energies on this planet. They have of course many times come to work with souls on the earth to help it to evolve. They come with great love for mankind because without love nothing can evolve.

Since our last contact your vibrations have shifted and not alone that but I'm happy to say that the vibrations of the whole planet earth has shifted as well. This of course makes our contact much easier this time round. In the many new age books as they are called which are around today including this one, which clearly states that the universe provides; this is true. However, the problem with all of this is the lack of trust, you see people on earth have for so long been giving away their soul power to outside source's within many controlled organisations church, state and social structures. One would say that that was fine as it kept people on the straight and narrow, which is very true, but this system has also kept us from moving forward as it interfered with the law of free will. There is a major shift in vibrations of the planet at present and this can be easily seen all over the world. Structures that were so long in place and which one would think were built with walls of steel are now starting to show cracks and are now starting to crumble. This I hope will make people more aware that no thing or states can be ruled by one so called belief system. The British royal family I mention here as they say in your "world watch this space". The British royal family will experience another blow that will truly rock their world. These shifts will continue for some time which all depends on peoples awareness and will seem very confusing times indeed. As people connect again to their true essence, which is happening at present on your earth through the many forms of alternative live style this shift can be speeded up, ten fold. This is what is really happening at present people are studying various types of meditation etc which will stop them searching outside of themselves and they will look inward for the true essence. (See chamber of connections)

As regards to these chambers there are nine chambers in all. The chamber of council of love and light governs them all. This chamber oversee all that is going on in this galaxy and oversees the transformation and transcending of souls in and out of this planet Arcturus and other worlds. They also oversee the transformation and awareness of human's evolution from third vibrations to the seventh. They are closely linked to other galaxies like Sirius and Pleiades who are keeping a close eye on earth and keeping it infused with rays of light so that the planet doesn't self-destruct. These planets I talk about are part of the universe but a universe that science has not yet recognised as these planets are of the inner worlds and of the inner universe and not of the three dimensional universe. Up to now, only a little ray of energy could get through but with the shift in awareness' and vibrations the planet earth is getting high voltages of subdued light every six months in earth terms. Also as I mentioned earlier many of the ascended masters like Christ are working closely with your lightworkers at present. They are working from the realm of places like Fintorn, Fatima, Stonehenge and Arizona USA and they are working in the exoteric realms or inner realms. Ireland and British Isles are to be the focal point for this great shift and if you look around you will see evidence of this everywhere. Everywhere there are rapid changes such as church, state and social changes and of course technology just to mention a few. Many people are searching and regaining their power through the connection with the many lightworkers that have chosen Ireland and the British Isles to work from.

When we were in contact the last time you were slow to move into the fifth vibration, as indeed was everyone else but because of your voluntary work as a lightworker and your practice of meditation you made the shift just at the right time. That's another law of the universe that everything happens at the right time, but this will be all explained in grater detail as we go into the different chambers. I said that there were nine chambers in all and they are sub divided into cells. I mentioned earlier that I (being your spiritual guide that you have been listening to throughout this introduction); who comes from the chamber of love and light, which oversees the working of all the other chambers, nine in all. Forgive me if I repeat myself here; but there is so much information that I want to disclose to you through this book "The Power To Connect" so this information will be made available to everyone who seeks it out.

The chambers are controlled by women or the female energy. Now, don't get me wrong here women do not control men as there is no battle of the sexes here on Arcturus, not like Earth.

The female energy is held in high esteem and in the future this energy is also going to be held in high esteem on earth.

At present the female energy is raising and making the transition much easier as women are moving into higher places both within council, state and very shortly the church.

Greetings.

Foreword

The mind is the key to all worlds, to this world and the next i.e. the inner world. Everything is created in the mind by using imagination and visualization, which creates feelings and emotion; we create the world we want to live in. This is known as the second coming or Christ consciousness, when we can create Heaven on Earth. This is brought about by the shift in consciousness from third vibration to seventh vibration. Many will get through this transition and many will get caught up or stuck somewhere between what they think is real and what is not. As I said this planet has taken at present a huge leap from the third dimensional to fifth dimensional with some catastrophic consequences and some yet to be seen. Scientists are calling this climate change but of course this goes much deeper that climate change. However climate change is indeed the result of the vibrations shifting both with the earth and within everything that inhabits it. Nothing new here perhaps, as the earth is prone to change every couple of thousands years or so. However this time round evolution is moving faster now that ever before, perceived by most of us by the passing of time. One day it's spring the next day it's Xmas, one day you're a young child and the next you're an adult. It feels now somehow that in people's lives that they have lived two or three life times in the one lifetime. This is because of the vibrational shift of the planet and interplanetary forces. Everything is vibration and moving at very fast speeds and we humans find it hard to connect or keep up with all of this in a 3-D reality. We need now more than ever in human evolution, to find quiet time for spirit, to go inwards to our subconscious minds. Then we can discover multi dimensional realities so we can transcend to a higher frequency of a multi-dimensional time frame. To get a clear picture on all of this we need to meditate and go to our inner word of imagination, visualization. We need now, more than ever to learn some skills of meditation and find quiet time for the spirit to strengthen us physically, mentally and spiritually.

In the continuous practice of meditation the vibrational rate of a person or persons and energy counterparts cells, molecules and atoms etc are raised and transmuted to a much higher frequency. This is not something anyone tries to consciously achieve, it just happens. This is why the old Masters referred to the practice of meditation as receiving grace i.e. "food for spirit". Because of the relaxed frame of mind and controlled breathing in meditation the cells molecules and atoms of the body are recharged with life giving energy, the life force that's within us all. This is the force that makes people, dogs or cats etc out of jumble of Hydrogen, Carbon, Nitrogen and Oxygen Atoms. This is the force that makes life out of inorganic substance, which has many names. The most common name is Chi (see chi energy) by the Chinese, Prana by the Indians and second generation of Hydrogen Atoms by modern western physicists all meaning the same thing but looked at from different angles by people with different social, religious, and spiritual backgrounds, but most certainly heading in the same direction.

Albert Einstein considered himself to be a very spiritual person and the more he studied the more he realised that there must be an organising force behind these processes that he was witnessing. Harry Edward called this organising force the body intelligence, which he believed was a separate intelligence apart from the mind to that of the brain (more on this later). Stephen Hawking arguably the finest theoretical physicist of our time regularly discussed "Gods" role in the scheme of things in his famous book "A Brief History in Time ". No going into too much details, all the energy on this planet today comes from either past or present solar activity and that all things in the universe are a creation of energy a jumble of Carbon, Hydrogen, Nitrogen and Oxygen Atoms or life force. We can enhance this life force within us by the continual practice of meditation.

In meditation the body regains it youthfulness in structure and indeed sometimes in appearance, so you may age seventy years but look and act fifty.

We are all far too caught up with age and the ageing process. We should perhaps not think in terms of numbers, or of years lived but we should think of life as essence that feeds constantly from within.

Meditation in all it's forms can be used to strengthen any organ or organ system of the body that may be deficient or weak and not functioning at 100% capacity. It can also be used to raise the general energy level of the person to relieve stress and to attune them to their surroundings and the world at large.

This is what meditation can do for us. Indeed there are many ways we can raise the vibration rate of our bodies and of the planet. This can be achieved through prayers, sound, dance, light, Tai Chi, Yoga, etc, as these are all good grounding tools and we should find stillness for spirit at least once a day, to allow the energy to recharge itself again. That means "time out" i.e. taking time out for ourselves. Any system or doctrine that will enhance the flow of energy and keep the Chakras spinning and healthy is fine. We are doing what the universes intended us to do and that is to allow the energy to flow in and out unconditionally from the physical body to other persons, from the cosmic to the earth and from the earth to the physical. I said earlier that we can create the world we want to live in by the power of our mind and I also said that this is brought about by imagination and visualization of our thoughts and or feelings, simple but powerful and may sometimes seem magical.

The late Betty Shine a truly remarkable woman and one of the worlds renowned healers addresses this subject very well in her books " Mind Magic" and "Mind Waves", She and many like her since have brought the possibility of bringing mind magic into the physical realm like creating the world we want to live in by the power of the mind by understanding mind energy. In the American film "Star Trek" on one of their series took this issue a little further when a mad scientist and a dying alien propelled the enterprise at wrap speed a billion light years away to a bizarre galaxy outside their own galaxy where their very thought turned into reality. Everything they thought of with strong emotion became reality at least for a short period of time. Of course this showed a down side to it as some of the crewmembers created their reality out of fear and doubt, what a pity.

Anything will only last as long as we give it the energy or thought to keep it in our present reality. So whatever we think about good or bad we attract into our lives. This is known as the law of attraction; more on this later.

However, magical and all as this world would seem to be, we do not live in a fairy tale world. I know that some would say that our imagination is the greatest gift of all and for all time and that is correct but we still must be careful not to let our imagination run amuck. We must be practical in all things and keep our feet firmly on the ground. What we have to learn, is to control our imagination and learn to concentrate and live every moment in the now. Every thought, visualisation and inspiration does not come from the brain or perhaps the physical mind but comes from the very depths of our being, our spiritual mind, that part of us that connects us to our higher- self or what perhaps should be called the inner self. Everything that is now and always will be; has always been and is connected to the source i.e. the God within. There is no name for this as everyone will have their own names from whatever level of awareness their mind is at. Everyone will put their own slant to it. There are many heavens or hells or what we now call the Astral worlds more on this later. For now it is suffice to say that everything and everyone are existing at a particular degree of vibration exhibiting similar characteristics in accordance with the vibration of whatever plane of existence or dimension they are at in this dimension or the next (Astral Worlds). "There are many rooms in my father house", many levels of awareness and many states of mind. Indeed this is not a place, however this is very real. All beings after physical death transcend to the astral world matching his/her particular energy, ego, temperament, character, vibration, beliefs and attitudes. On the time of physical death, as was pointed out in my book "A way To Healing

The Seven Set Practice" to barrow a phrase, " as man think so shall he be ".

Imagination may be the greatest gift of all and of all times but it must be kept within control. So don't use your imagination to escape into a fairy tale world to escape from the world you're in, but rather use your imagination to enhance and create your own reality. Use your imagination to bring you inward to the very depths of your being and to remove you from the illusion of incarnated life on earth and to help you to realise that heaven is truly within. Even though it has taken thousands of earthly years of evolution to reach this far and now at this present time in our evolutionary history we are beginning to understand the true reality of life itself and perhaps the destiny of mankind. It should be stated here however that the entire universe, which is the spiritual universe, the seven dimension, there are no borders or boundaries between this world and the next i.e. the Astral worlds. The entire universe from the highest esoteric substance to the lowest vibration of physical matter is continual and consisting of infinitive energy and vibrations.

To conclude; *I do believe the time is coming when we will regard everything in the universe as being one – the essence without fear or judgement which will radiate through us, bringing a shift to our physical vibrations, healing to those areas we need and the planet as a whole. This all goes down to working with energy and vibrations. Indeed the vibrational rate of the planet itself is rising and there are those that will go with it and those that will not.*

Those that will are in tune with their higher energy, they are also in tune with the higher vibration rate of things and people around them. In short, they are in tune with the pleasant things in life, love, compassion, the colours of the trees and sky above them or the magnificence of a sunrise or sunset. They are in harmony with the world around them and they have achieved the art of being. This raising awareness and use of energy will eventually lead to enlightenment for us all, and physics and science plays its part as we move from Piscean age to Aquarian age. In this Aquarian age, we are transmuting in many ways, with the vibration of our spiritual and intellectual minds, moving into higher gears as we evolve. In such hectic times, we hunger for meaning and guidance, but often don't have the time or the patience to pause and reflect deeply on our situation or our perceptions.

However many people are aware of a shift in consciousness at present on our planet and that we are at a time now in our evolution, not just as actors acting out our parts on this stage we call the earth but as the script writers, co-producers and co-directors of the final outcome.

This new awareness' will undoubtedly change a person's perception of the world, life and the very meaning of life itself. It will help us all to transcend into the next vibration of our choosing I hope that we choose wisely and avoid the pitfalls of past.

I know that there's much work and teaching to be done to make this shift as easy as possible and for as many people as possible. I do hope that this book in some small way can help towards that work.

Finally let us all come together and expand the ultimate collective consciousness of our minds; thoughts, words, deeds and actions by the power of our imagination, meditation and visualisation and create the world we want live in.

As Einstein once said, "that intelligence is great but imagination is everything".

Greetings

Chapter I

Chamber of Council

We start with the chamber of council or guides and high priests that oversee everything. Just as there are order and laws in the physical world there are also order and laws in astral or spirit world, which from now on I will refer to as the seventh vibration/ seven vibrations. Because the spirit world has many worlds everyone that passes over to spirit go as many would say to the spirit world. Death is a natural process of life or a continuation of life. Everyone passes over rich and poor, good and bad, all religions but not all live together as like will follow like. Thankfully the lower vibrations do not mix with the higher vibrations. There are vibrations where souls are suffering the remorse of retribution for acts of conscious harm they were responsible for in other life times. They will stay in this vibration until their level of awareness shifts by some Divine act. This of course could take eternity in terms of earth's years, who knows? So souls of a lower awareness will go to a lower vibration, i.e. the lower astral worlds. Some will choose to go back to earth, but those souls, would have not yet reached the seventh vibration, or indeed the fourth vibration. However some choose to stay with like kind on the lower vibrations, their hell if you like, because we have all got free will. That is the one law that all vibrations have in common known as universal law and is really quite simple what you give out you get back and as you think so you are (see the laws of attractions). For instance if a person passes on to the lower astral world after committing horrible acts of murder and other acts of violence's they will find themselves in a dimension where they are with other souls who want to murder them. They will continue to murder others in the same way and this state of awareness can go on for an eternity in earthly time, as there is no such thing as time in the lower astral worlds. Or course they will not be able to harm anyone as there can be no killing in the Astral worlds. However the drama leading up to the actual murder will continue for that person until some act of remorse, which will shift their conscience and bring them out of this dark vibration. Then they can eventually be reincarnated back to earth or transcend to another world in the universe, the choice is theirs. I should like to state here that the universe I'm talking about here is not the physical universe but the spirit or inner planes of the universe. Anyone who has mastered astral travel will fully understand this, (see astral travel).

One must remember that all things are forms of energy which combine all vibrations and that nothing exists without a purpose. So the chamber of council oversees everything in all dimensions and I said they are divided into nine other chambers which we will discus separately but now back to the chamber of council.

To get an understanding of how the council operates we must first explain a little about time, time in the sense of your world, but as already stated there is no time only the speed band in which you operate. If one were to travel into the past that time in the present would seem like hours or perhaps days or weeks depending how far back we travel but if one were to travel into the future that time in present would seem like seconds. Stephen Hawking refers to this possibility as a black hole. However, in the chamber council and indeed all chambers it is referred to as a vortex. A vortex is created from spiralling motion of air, liquid or gas around a centre of rotation, if you have ever watched water going down your sink then you have seen a vortex but more on this later. The main vortex is operated from the chamber of council and everything on a universal scale is seen from this vortex. This vortex is one that allows the collective consciousness, that holds negative energy to be distinguished from collective consciousness that holds the positive energy. This vortex clears the energy of the planetary system of the past, present and future events, but as already said there is no time here. Time is measured if you like by progression, but the members of this council have a strong interest in earth at its present evolution which is moving faster today than the wheel of a automobile. It is from this chamber that the 37 councillors or ascended Master send love and light to other worlds and of course to the earth. The best known of these masters to you is Jesus Christ or known in the inner worlds as Lord Sananda. Christ came unto earth 2000 years ago carrying the sixth rays of energy embodied in Christ, which was to do with marriage, devotion and idealism. Although the sixth rays of energy is moving off the planet as we speak, as it is no longer needed. Today the seventh energy that is to do with self -empowerment and purification is very active on the planet at present. The seventh energy is to do with self empowerment which is the main topic of today's world everywhere you look there are self empowerment workshops, books, videos, DVD's, web sites not to mention my own, which are totally geared to this purpose. In fact some reference and quotes in this book are taken from TVE Cosmic Internet Academy and I am thankful for their permission., and a special word of appreciation to Sarah Alexander for her permission on reference's and quotes on pages 95/ 96 of this book, I would advise anyone to look them up, fascinating stuff indeed (see web sites below),

However at this point I would like to stress that 90% of this book is inspirational and 10% of it is with reference and research, mainly from my other works and the websites below.

www.selfempowermenacademy.com,
www.thelightweaverway.co.za.
www.paradigmshift
www.sarah-alexander.co.uk

So as self-empowerment and purification is the flavour of the month, this energy came about towards the beginning of the millennium and is associated with St Germain and Merlin the magician. They work from the chamber of council and work along side the lightworkers on the planet earth at present and are associated with places like Fatima, working of course in the inner realms; Fatima yes; but a world within worlds as in the seventh vibration there are no separations but we will look at this in more detail later on.

To get a better understanding of these vibrations let us look at how these vibrations have come to our planet and are still coming to our planet at the present time. Today the seven vibrations are most active on our planet. These vibrations are sent to the earth from the higher vibrations of love and light, controlled by the chamber of council at different period of time and history to help it evolve. We are indeed extensions of the earth's energy and we have received this energy into our bodies through the Chakra system (see Chakra) to help us evolve and transcend further and further into the light or higher vibrations. This process is now speeded up a hundred fold at present on our planet and with the law of nature sometimes things seem worse before they get better. Just like nature the centre of the storm has to find it's own balance. But because we humans are an extension of the earth we play an important part in bringing the balance about even through our thoughts, words and deed because everything and all vibrations work on energy even our thoughts. The universal law states what you give out you get back as we can see from our actions of the last century of the industrial age. We have dumped so much rubbish into the atmosphere we will receive back, a hundred times that amount. Mankind is not alone and we will learn from our mistakes no matter how long this takes. There is an enormous shift of consciousness on the planet at present. The higher vibrations are bombarding us with cosmic rays every six to eight months to raise the awareness of the damage we have inflicted on ourselves by the separation of me from you or from them to us. Thankfully through the great work of the lightsworkers in all walks of life, we humans are raising our awareness by our thoughts, words, deeds and actions to make this a better place for our children and our grand children. This is known as Christ like consciousness, the shift into the seven vibrations. As the different energies come to the planet we are also affected because as I said earlier we are extensions of the earth energies. I will be talking mostly here about the seven energy or the seventh vibration because that is where were at, at the present. Although not everybody has evolved to this vibration yet as another law of the universe states that everything happens in it's own time and at the correct time. The chamber of council controls all this. Although not everything is written in stone, though some things are, back to the energies.

Now we will look at the different energies on our planet and how they came in at different times through history etc. and how they also affect our own body energy centres as well, which I mention briefly in my last book "A Way To Healing The Seven Set Practice".

ENERGIES OF THE PLANET

The seven energy centres in the body are related to the seven energies that have come into the planet.

The first energy is to do with will, power and action and vibrates to the colour of red.

The second energy, which is deep blue, which is helping our planet to evolve now, is to do with love and wisdom.

The third energy is green and is to do with, using your mental process to get the will of God grounded on earth.

The fourth energy is yellow and is to do with the arts, music, dance, writing, film etc. It is still with us, but it came in very strong in the turn of the last century as the world had very dark vibrations at that time.

The fifth energy, which is orange, is to do with the new age, which has got much stronger since the new Millennium.

Teaching us to use our mental powers and bring forth new skills and scientific development.

The sixth energy is the Christ like energy which is indigo it came in 2000 years ago embodied in Christ. It stands for religion, idealism and devotion. It is now moving away as it is no longer needed. This time there is more emphasis on the seven rays to do with purification and self-empowerment and oneness with spirit.

The seventh energy is to do with the purple ray of purification and healing and it is most active on the planet as we speak.

There is an eight energy, which is white, which I know very little about, other than it is a deep cleansing energy. All I do know is that we are getting a chance of coming out of the dark and heavy vibrations of the past and moving into light vibrations with total balance of Yin and Yang.

The seventh energy is a mixing of both male and female energy male being blue and female being pink, so the mixing of the two gives us purple. This is known as the purple flame and is manifested through St Germaine, which tells us to use the violet/purple flame of freedom. Welcome it into every atom and cell of your body and world. Each day ask your God Presence for greater Wisdom and for an increase of the flame of illumination and its right use.

You will see many lightworkers wearing purple to enhance their aura or magnetic field. Purple of course through history was and still is a spiritual colour. This colour plays an important part in healing and vibrations and more so in the seventh vibration (see the camber of healing).

Self-empowerment really means stepping into your own power and not giving it away to any groups social, religious, state or otherwise. However, that doesn't mean that you should not be part of a group as no man is an island. What it means is that you take part in the group rather than belong to the group.

In the same way as you are part of your family but you do not belong to your family or better still your family does not own you. A husband does not own his wife or a wife own a husband or a father own a son etc. This is what self - empowerment is all about. To be self-empowered one can still belong and take an active part but one to should have total independence and freedom within their group. Everyone is allowed to make up their own minds on ideas and beliefs rather than following some dogma or tradition, in other words; one is totally independent in finding his or her truth. In the seventh vibration there are many truths, many realities and many possibilities; the problem on earth is finding yours. In the purple rays of energy that is active on our planet at present, (the seventh vibration) man is given back his independence and freedom on many levels as the shift in awareness comes about. He will no longer need any doctrine book or Bible, Karan or Ten Commandments to tell him when he is doing right or wrong. He will have reached awareness that; he only wants to do loving positive acts for the glory and grace of all. When you were a child you thought like a child but now you're a man you put away your childlike ways and think like a man in other words in the seven vibration we think and act the truth according to our awareness. We put away the ignorance of the past, the third vibration which was associated with the solar plexus charka, which is to do with courage and strength and dogma wars etc. As we move into the fourth /seventh vibration we think with the heart Chakra which is to do with unconditional love and courage again, only this time the courage comes from compassion and love and not from fear and ego either religious or superstitious. Evidence of this can be seen all over the world as the old hard ways of the past are going and more peaceful relaxed ways are approaching. More and more souls are evolving through the heart Chakra by compassion and this is having a tremendous affect on our planet, because without love nothing can evolve.

As we have learned to move the energy up through the Chakra system in the body. The earth, which is a living breathing organism, is also moving the energy up through its Chakra system and we are now in a position to leave the old way behind. So in the seventh vibration everyone is connected on a collective conscious level without fear of judgment. The purple flame of purification has brought this about i.e. if we want it to as everything is governed by the laws of the universe, mainly the law of cause and effect. As we make this shift in conscious with the help of the ascended master it is important that we meditate. By the skills of meditation and visualisation we can project our energy by the power of the mind. This will create the world we want to live in, in other words to create the seventh vibration here on earth (heaven on earth). This is why so many lightworks are associated with Masters from other chambers guided by the Chamber of Council, to move this planet into the seventh vibration. This is why today time does surely seem to have speeded up. Time as we know has no relevance, its just that vibrations have shifted, that is all. In the seventh vibration there is no such thing as time or space only the speed ban or belt that we are at, or we are vibrating at. That is why so many lightworkers are able to see relatives that have passed on, possibly to the fifth, sixth or seventh vibration. I said in my last book "A Way to Healing", those on the forth vibration will stay there until everything is in order or will perhaps be reborn again on earth. Their vibration does not go anywhere, just adapt another body guided again by the Chamber of Council or perhaps their vibration will re establish itself on other worlds depending on it's soul journey, which ever is better for them. So you see it really is worlds within worlds and this is the task of the Chamber of Council so that everything runs smoothly within the laws of free will. As not everything is written in stone though some events are, again it's all a matter of the principle of the law cause and effect.

"Every Cause has its Effect; every Effect has its Cause;everything happens according to the law.

The law of Chance is but a name for Law not recognized; as there are many planes of causation, but nothing escapes the Law"

This Principle embodies the fact that there is a Cause for every Effect; an Effect from every Cause. It explains that: "Everything Happens according to Law"; that nothing ever "merely happens"; there is no such thing as Chance; that while there are various planes of Cause and Effect, the higher dominating- the lower planes, nothing ever entirely escapes the Law".

Many ancient civilizations understood the art and methods of rising above the ordinary plane of Cause and Effect, to a certain degree, and by mentally rising to a higher plane they become Causers instead of Effectors. However, the masses of people are carried along, obedient to environment; the wills and desires of others stronger than themselves; heredity; suggestion; and other outward causes moving them about like pawns on the Chessboard of Life. But the Masters, rising to the plane above, dominate their moods, characters, qualities, and powers, as well as the environment surrounding them, and become movers instead of pawns.

According to this law of cause and effect, every thought, word and deed sets up an immediate chain of causation, on every plane to which this chain reaches. When we acknowledge this law we can test it, prove it to ourselves and then mould our lives accordingly.

We can resolve past, present and future karmic ties by current action using thought, will and intention and we can free ourselves of such influences at will by understanding and applying other universal laws which I have also covered briefly in my book, "A Way to Healing" probably the most crucial law is the Drama of reincarnation which is about the Drama or the illusion of life where Drama is the essence of it all.

To those still unaware of such powers, how do you explain that all that occurs in life on earth is to do with karma and Drama? To understand that our attitudes and awareness come not just from genetic and environmental influences, but from the influences of past, present and future lives? To understand that universal law keeps everything in alignment with the cosmic plan of creation and that the mirth in the mastery is that we can stay on the wheel of life and death for as long as we wish since we create it all anyway. We will talk more about this later but now it's suffice to say that all life, spirit and matter is governed by universal law and we as Individuals have the power under universal law to create any reality that we desire - consciously or unconsciously.

We live in the plane of duality, a sea of endless time where all life is governed by the universal law of cause and effect. Buddha provided the eightfold path to free man from their suffering. "Right belief, right resolve, right speech, right behavior, right occupation, right effort, right contemplation, right concentration." Christian belief provided the Ten Commandments as a recipe for freedom from suffering and all the Masters of all world religions have provided a code yet sadly not many have the wisdom and understanding for such codes.

Greetings

Chapter 2

Chamber of Wisdom & Understanding

In the seventh vibration, the main tool of progression is wisdom and understanding a code of value which were so completely opposed to those values on earth until the last shift in awareness which took place at the start of this new millennium. Wisdom and understanding is only starting to become part of the earth existence at the present time and remember only yet part of awareness for those of you who have moved to the seventh vibration. There are still those on the earth stuck in the third vibration of ignorance. This awareness of spirit has always been around and on the planet but only for a few. As time evolved more and more souls became aware of the shift in conscience and not just such souls like Betty Shine, Harry Edwards, Diane Cooper and Doreen Virtue to mention a few who have pioneered the mediumship of the last couple of decades. It is now possible for everyone to evolve and transcend in awareness (see chapter transformation transcend).

In the seventh vibration life in the future world from where we come is different. It is civilized. There is no war, no slaughter of animal or human life. People live on Divine Chi Power, are fed and nourished by its light. Food is consumed only for pleasure and world hunger has long been solved - partly due to the work of the lightworkers of today and the seeds they have now planted. This is partly due to an increase in awareness among certain groups that control food distribution and political decision making in this area. In this future world which I have refereed to all throughout this book as being the seventh vibration; people never get sick as they understand that they are systems of energy that can easily be retuned. Time spent in silence - in meditation and contemplation - is honoured and encouraged, and part of holistic education. (See the new hospitals in China in chamber of healing and guides).

There is no such thing, as poverty, for everyone knows about Universal Laws and how to manifest what they desire to take care of creature comforts. People can come and go from their bodies at will, many work multi-dimensionally and cross the lines of time as they have discovered and accepted that past, present and future co-exist and accessing time lines is a matter of personal and environmental frequency adjustment, an ability that comes from lifestyle choice. Between now and the future that the time travellers come from, we as a species on earth learn not just to cure current diseases, but also how to prevent future ones. Alternative and traditional medicines merge and combine forces and using holistic education, stimulate great changes in awareness levels and personal responsibility levels of the individual. In other words, doctors cease to be Gods and people stop giving away their power seeking symptomatic cures and feeding the drug companies their billions. Drug companies therefore, are free to expand into other areas of research and still make their billions and people become self empowered.

Between now and then, medical research moves and goes towards a genetic level, free from the needs to focus on cures for disease that can be avoided through preventative medicine. Preventative medicine lifestyles and techniques are taught in homes and in educational packages that are made freely available to all. Between now and then schools disappear and education is done via the Internet, i.e. the power to connect at home, to cater for the new generation's desire for limitless learning, i.e. the Indigo children, cooperation replaces competition. Between now and then quantum mechanics and metaphysics which automatically bridge science, healing and religion to the satisfaction of all.

Between now and then earth's people discover intergalactic civilisations, a sort of 'Star Trek' mode, and we, as a species become much more humble as we begin to intermingle with civilisations far more advanced than our own. Earth becomes part of the Intergalactic Federation of Worlds and has representatives on the Governing Chamber of Council just as countries have representatives at the United Nations today. All these things will become evident in time and so the lightworkers living in this time need great patience, as they plant the seeds of these possibilities to inspire humanity to unify and become civilised and worthy of being on the galactic stage.

Some of you may read these words and ask when will this occur? Firstly, when all this will occur is dependent on only one thing - how soon humanity decides as individuals to create personal lifestyles that will allow them access to Divine Chi Power. Once this Power is flowing and personal paradise has been created and enjoyed, it depends on how soon we can unify and implement holistic education (including the benefits of Divine Chi Power) so that the masses can eliminate personal stumbling blocks like ego, fear, power issues around sex, fame or money (which are the current Gods being worshipped in the Western world. The Western world is where the wealth lies, and the current most dominant power source on the global scene is the USA with Europe and Japan trailing.

Between now and then, leaders in political, social, education and environmental arenas will undergo a personal awakening to Divine Chi Power or be phased out and replaced by those who have. This will result in gradual redistribution of the world's resources in a way that honours all.

Also, I would like to clarify that there are many lightworkers now living and influencing world affairs. However, they come from different time spans and for different purposes. Under universal law, influence must be done in alignment with free will and also in a manner that mirrors the Divine Plan.

1. On earth the free will game is where people are learning how to co-create realities beyond survival. This includes the general state of amnesia where people still think they are just their mind, body and emotions, or where there are still driven by personal agendas that see them worshipping or dealing with the Gods called fame, sex, money or power etc.

2. The other field is the Divine will game that attracts the metaphysicians and the religiously aware who have no doubt about the existence of the supreme force of intelligence that is the source and governing force of all creation.

3. Then we have the multitudes that transition between the games feeling there is more but not yet awake, via personal experience, to Divine Chi Power. Some in the Divine will game carry their baggage of beliefs about external Gods and right or wrong ways and judge and/or kill in the name of God. Religious wars have hounded earth for millennia.

Each game has numerous personalities playing within it. On earth 6 billion people play within these games, aware or unaware, but still pawns to a greater or lesser degree. The main attribute of the free will game is that any reality is plausible and possible, and that each individual is the centre of their universe, the leading man or lady, the scriptwriter, producer and director of their final outcome.

Both the free will game that is responsible for the chaos and the Divine Will game that reveals the order behind the chaos, exist according to the dictates of certain laws of creation -

Universal Laws. These laws are non-manipulate and will be obeyed consciously or not, and part of the art of making the free will game easier, is to discover how these laws operate and then apply them. This is something that, according to the BBC "Time Lords" program, those in quantum physics have also begun to understand.

Back to why some come from the future and merge with earlier versions of themselves. The answer is to influence the future of our world today. Those that wish to be influenced and play the Divine Will game, will in turn influence others susceptible to wanting to exist in a reality where all life is honoured and looked after, and thus a parallel reality is born. Similar to what James Redford talks about in 'The Celestine Prophecy'.

So the future world that those serving come from, is a world where the Divine Plan has unfolded and is continuing to unfold and is being consciously supported by its inhabitants, and yes this world exists right now in a parallel universe, i.e. the seventh vibration.

The Law of Attraction

We all work with one infinite power. We all guide ourselves by exactly the same laws. The natural laws of The Universe are so precise that we don't even have any difficulty building spaceships; we can send people to the moon, and we can time the landing with the precision of a fraction of a second
Wherever you are - India, Australia, New Zealand, Stockholm, London, Toronto, Montreal, or New York - we're all working with one power. One law. It's the Law of Attraction!

The Secret is The Law of Attraction;

Everything that's coming into your life, you are attracting into your life. And it's attracted by virtue of the images you're holding in your mind. It's what you're thinking. Whatever is going on in your mind, you are attracting to you.

To understand the Law of Attraction, let's first understand its underlying counterpart, The Law of Vibration. The Law of Vibration states that EVERYTHING vibrates (everything moves). Everything ever created from the smallest atomic particle to the largest skyscraper is in a constant state of energetic motion. What looks solid is not, even concrete, glass and steel is energy in constant motion (see quantum physic).

We live in an ocean of motion;

What this lesson teaches us is that you have a power within you that is far superior to any circumstance or situation around you – you have free will over what you want to think. And these are the very thoughts that are in charge of directing power to whatever you choose in your lifetime.

But here is the thing you need to understand; Unconscious Attraction and Conscious Attraction, whatever you think about, whether it's good or bad - you attract into your life. Whether you want it or not is irrelevant - think about something you don't want and you attract it into your life this is the law of attraction and people are starting to gain more knowledge of this law and this knowledge will expand the consciousness of man and catapult us into the seventh vibration.

Greetings

Chapter 3

Chamber of Knowledge

Yes it's true that if you expand the consciousness of an individual so that they undergo Divine transformation of experiencing and emerging in the Divine nature of God within then this will naturally transform and expand the consciousness of the whole world.

The wise once said that a little knowledge is dangerous and in the same breath they said that ignorance is the sole cause of all our problems. There are two ways of looking at this; if one has little knowledge of something and they start to tamper with it they probably do more harm that good. However, on the other hand ignorance is perhaps a great many causes of all the darkness in the world today because what man didn't understand he tried to conquer, control or kill. So knowledge is the key to the seven vibrations and the more that science evolves the faster we can achieve this shift. When you think about it; it took us almost two thousand years to reach this far but as I said this will no longer be the case as evolution is shifting faster now than the wheel of an automobile. So as we move into the fifth vibration and as some of us are already in the seventh vibration, there's no argument to say that one is better than the other no matter what vibration they're in. Remember its all a question of awareness. The only way we can have more awareness is through knowledge and through wise minds, which are working with like-minded people on the fifth vibration and who will very shortly emerge into the seventh vibration. In this chamber all knowledge from the beginning of time is stored. Think of it for now as a vast computer of a vast mind or indeed all mind i.e. God. To put a little more perspective on all of this lets go back and talk about planetary systems and lots more. After all this is the chamber of knowledge and all knowledge is available to everyone in the seven vibrations.

There is between 100 billion to 400 billion stars in your galaxy the Milky Way which is just one of the 140 billion other galaxies. Many of these stars are bigger that earth and have planetary system that are also habitable which makes earth if you like, one of millions of advanced civilizations. The distance between these advance civilizations is approximately 200 light years. If we could go in a space ship like the enterprise it would take approximately 25,000 years to reach our nearest neighbour in the cosmos, which is 43 light years away. As you know in this realm which is the physical realm which has three dimensions of space and one of time, hence the third dimension which according to Stephen Hawking are interconnected and interwoven like treads woven together on a piece of cloths. This of course is known as quantum physics that supports that the metaphysical principle that we are all interconnected and that we are all one, and that time is ever-changing, variable and has shape. This is the theory of relativity that says that space and time are absolute to the observer and to that of which is been observed. So you see time can run simultaneously in metaphysical world seven vibrations and the material world third vibrations. A thought is only real because it has been observed. Keep this in mind the next time a negative thought comes to you, don't give it any power to manifest by observing it, it will so vanish as if it was never there, remember you created it in the first place by the power of your mind.

Sciences would ask us to understand the concept of 'space time' by imagining a heavy object or ball rolling on the surface of a stretched out rubber cloth and how it curves this rubber cloth with its weight. If you then roll a smaller ball across this fabric in a straight line, as it nears the larger ball it will automatically curve itself downward to the bigger ball. Science calls this gravity or the bending of space-time. Every object in our cosmos creates a little indentation in the fabric of space-time.

The upshot of all this for most people is that we live in a universe, surrounded by stars whose distances from us and each other we don't altogether know, filled with matter we can't identify, operating within physical laws whose properties we don't truly understand.

Human beings are as we said an energy form made up of the jumble of hydrogen atoms and we know that energy cannot be destroyed or created. It can only be transformed or change form, and because of this law human beings have an eternal energy which we call the spirit and which you have now come to know in the seventh vibration as physical immortality. Regardless of physical immortality, our spirit, or inner being goes on forever in another form.

However humans in the third dimension are still slaves to time and they forget to feed their inner spirit the nourishment from time spent in a timeless world of meditation of essence and source of life or Chi energy (see chi energy).

This timeless world is not about putting things off, or being irresponsible, or living anywhere but the now.

Meditation simply grounds us and puts things into a bigger perspective thus allowing us to rest and fully appreciate each moment to have an attitude and understanding of the eternal nature of existence and the vastness of who we are, and that we exists beyond time and space and man made time restrictions. This so called freedom we get through meditation, is not something new or just discovered but its a concept we all already have, if for now perhaps hidden away in our subconscious mind. The planet at this particular time in evolution is going through one of its biggest changes since Newton's time (where everything was thought as being of the mechanical structure and operated like clockwork). As we now know with the advance in the 21st century science and physic by the great leader in the field of quantum physicist Einstein, Bolmont, Stephen Hawking and the likes. We know now that everything and all matter is energy. Scientists discovered that the so-called 'subatomic particles' were not particles at all. They behaved like particles when they were measured but they traveled like waves.

This indeed is by far the biggest mind shift we humans have to make since we discovered the world was round. The more people are educated to this theory the more this theory will help in human evolution and help us to shift to the seventh vibration. This however is not enough, humans must discover and experience this for themselves, and this will only happen at a collective level. When more and more minds open up to this concept, not just alone through teaching or guru, but through the experience and understanding that everything is energy and it is only made real by the observer. Stop observing it and it becomes a wave of energy again. This is quantum physics and this is to be known as the quantum age. What quantum psychics simply means is, if we look closely under a microscope at an object e.g. a car, TV, computer it would appear that they're not solid at all but are composed of quantum /energy moving and vibrating at a very high rate in and out of the object i.e. TV, car etc being observed.

However real and external they may seem, these constructions are all phenomena within the mind. It seems undeniable that out there, around us, independent and apart from us, exists a physical world, utterly real, solid and tangible. But the world of our experience is no more out there than are our dreams. When we dream, we create a reality in which events happen around us, and in which we perceive other people as individuals separate from us. In the dream it all seems very real. But when we awaken we realize that everything in the dream was actually a creation of our own mind. Time, space, and matter are secondary. They are aspects of an image of reality manifesting in the mind. They exist within consciousness; not the other way around.

We have at this present time on our planet all the resources to help this process and to move us into seven vibrations. Technology will surely play a major part in this process as the internet gives us all the power to connect on a much higher scale than perhaps the day of communication by pony express. Nothing is hidden from anyone any more. The world is watching; and as we make the shift into the seventh vibration this will have it's good points as well as it's bad points. Until man respects and trusts the privacy of his fellow man the good side to all or new technology is that yes, the world is watching and man will be caught out on his /her inhumane ways. Indeed we will have to pay back what he/ she has robbed from society by destroying and harming another soul.

In future every man that has not made this shift in humans' consciences for whatever reason will have to pay for his /her crime because in the seventh vibration there is no crime. This will all have to be dealt with in the fifth vibration. This is a not a question of locking up these souls and throwing away the key, we've tried that for the last hundred years and we have achieved nothing. The new system will work like this. As the planet shifts from one vibration to another men and woman in government and indeed church and state will understand that anyone who harms another human being will automatically be harming themselves. Nothing new here perhaps, this has been known for centuries, Jesus' who was of the sixth vibration when he was on earth spoke of this. When humans realize without a doubt that they create their own reality, crime will become a thing of the past. Of course there will be a system to help this process and at this time in human evolution the 37 chamber of council is discussing this process. People who commit a harmful deed will have to face the person they harm or the family's of them that they harm. This meeting will have enormous effect on each of them because the victim will have no anger or hatred towards their attacker due to the shift in there vibration and thinking and because they carry a great deal more (compassion) light that their attacker. You may remember I said earlier that there is no such thing as darkness in the seventh vibration, only the absence of light, the more light we can bring to the planet now the better and quicker the shift. Perhaps you may ask the question here; there seems to be a lot of darkness on the planet today as the news and papers are spreading bad stories all the time? For those of you who are in the third vibration this seems true. Those of you who have made this shift especially those of you who are at the seventh vibration will know otherwise. You will know and realize that the news is not real and cannot be real in the seventh vibration. This is why so much bad deeds are around at present, it's because as man thinks so shall he be. This is known as collective coconsciousness, but the more people operate in the mindset of the fifth vibration, the better for all. Then we can stop all this chaos and bring about a collective coconsciousness of the seventh vibration, in other words heaven on earth. This is known as the second coming or sometimes known as the Christ like coconsciousness. Many are expecting this to happen in the year 2012. This is foolish because in a way its happening now but the more we are educated and alter the educational system both church, state, science, medical and bring religion, science, superstition and medicine closer together, then we can all come together in a collective way and have peace for all reign once again on our planet.

We as a species at present are getting a lot of help from the higher Master and the Angelical realms. Those of you who are familiar with them. Michael the Archangel, Raphael the healer and the bringer of the seven rays or the purple rays of purification. Many of you may wonder why Michael the Archangel carries the sword, but do not look on the sword as a symbol of mass destruction but look on it as a symbol of truth and loyalty. It is a symbol; to cut away the ignorance and arrogance of the past in both religion and superstition, as one man's religion is another man's superstition, one equally as dangerous as the other. Both doctrines belong to the ego and both doctrines rule by control and fear and not out of compassion and freedom of the Spirit. With this freedom of Spirit, which is known as the Christ consciousnesses, we are now in the position to be, not alone the actor acting out our part on this stage the earth, but the script writers, co- producers and co-directors in the next stage of our evolution. In the seventh vibration through the Christ consciousness' each individual will come to know and understand the true meaning of "I and the father are one".

Greetings

Chapter 4

Chamber of Science

There is no such thing as a miracle as all things have a scientific explanation in the seventh vibration.

All things we have in common in this world and on the seventh vibration is form and as we know form is energy which as the law of physics says, energy cannot be destroyed or created. It is merely transformed from one source to another and everything is made up of energy i.e. an atom or a group of atoms. On earth at present the sciences have discovered around 200 atoms and have discovered a lot about the atom even so far as dividing the atom and producing the atomic bomb. Here on the seventh vibration however we have many more atoms. If a hydrogen atom could be enlarged to the size of the White House the nucleus inside it would be the size of a football and electrons around it would be no bigger that perhaps a golf ball. If one can visualise this for a moment one can perhaps get the picture of a tiny solar system. We know that if we joined two hydrogen atoms and one of oxygen we get a chemical substance called water or $H^{2}0$. We know if we joined two atoms together, we get a molecule. So it would be correct to say from this study that all sciences come. But man has always taken the negative approach in evolution, i.e. he chooses the tree of knowledge rather than the tree of life. The tree of life is a symbolic structure of 32 teachings of the Hebrew teaching known as the Kabbalah which goes back long before the pyramids were constructed and long before Christianity and other modern religions were formed. Although it's teachings are quite complex but at the very basic level it believes in total Divinity, i.e. that everything from the smallest physical world of matter to the larger inner spheres of spirit in the entire universe are all connected and are all one and the same. These teachings and philosophies span over the millennia that teaches Divine wisdom. These teachings unite all the great civilisations of east and west, Inca, Egyptian, Hebrew, including lost legendary civilisations of Atlantis and Lemuria which are no longer visible to the world due to environmental cataclysms and the action of man.

However, today evidence of these ancient civilisation is now beginning to emerge from the Atlantic and Pacific Oceans, so perhaps not quite as legendary as we might have thought and indeed not at all legendary in the seven vibrations. These civilisations teach that each and everyone is an immortal spirit made in the true image of God, however not as God in human form as widely believed by many religions but as God in immortal spirit. Scientist and indeed mankind in general have taken the long route to evolution and have chosen the tree of knowledge, which has led to many wars and almost the destruction of mankind. If we had to go with these teachings of many of the ancient civilisations of the past i.e. the tree of life, we would realise that not alone is God an immortal spirit but we are all immortal spirits made in the true image of God i.e. the source. The source here, being not of the orthodox dogmatic religious, but of the Ultimate Divinity, i.e. the universe itself. This might be somewhat a large statement to comprehend, but these beliefs go hand in hand with many ancient civilisations of the past and also go hand in hand with quantum physics of today's world, known as the quantum age, (see quantum physics).

So thankfully scientists are opening up to a new level of awareness and from this shift of collective coconscious a new science is about to be born. The knowledge and wisdom of ancient civilisations of the past were regarded as esoteric or hidden up to a few years ago and have been closely guarded and kept safe from those who were so hell bent on destroying everything. They did not succeed however. Mankind however was thrown into very dark times where greed dogma, oppression of orthodox religions became prevalent. Man has remained like this until such time has come about again when this ancient knowledge is made available for the benefit of mankind once more. Today this knowledge is no longer regarded as esoteric or hidden but is being more widely taught as the influence and power of the controlled orthodox religions diminishes. This is the awareness and the science of the seventh vibration. As I said these ancient civilisations were lost to the world many years ago and are no longer visible today. However, some evidence still remains of their existence and as we evolve, more and more evidence of these worlds will be discovered in the future, by new science technology and a collected mindset on science in general. So it is for the most part that science will catapult us into the seventh vibration i.e. quantum physic and indeed thanks to modern sciences, we can now get closer to the understanding and wisdom in how things are made in the seventh vibration. In a way we have to thank the atomic bomb.

So it would be fair to say that the fusion of two hydrogen atoms produces a molecule, but it would be also fair to say that it does not always produce a healthy outcome i.e. **the atomic bomb** as mentioned earlier some science have found out in the last century, this was the tree of knowledge. So it would also be fair to say that a hydrogen atom has an intelligence of its own as indeed all cells have an intelligence of their own i.e. they have their likes and dislikes. This was the belief that Harry Edwards had that made him understand the principle of all healing and giving him much success in his healings administrations but we will talk about this later. This is what science have yet to discover on earth. The hydrogen atom which I will refer from now on as a cell or cellular structure, is an agent not just suitable for its destructive nature but of its productive nature. This is what all science of the seventh vibration is based on, that all cells have a mind of their own and some are influenced by some forces but not others. It is the fusion of two hydrogen atoms or energy force, be it gravity, electricity, heat or light that all thing come to be in all dimensions. All life begins when energy forces become subjected to an inelegant directed force of thought obeying the natural law of cause and effect. Look at it like this we can put the forces of sound on glass and cause it to shatter or put the forces of heat on a stiff arthritic joint and we can see relief very quickly. As the calcium carbonate molecules melt down, breaking away, and freeing the client's joints. We will look at this in more detail in the chamber of healing and guides.

So everything in the universe has form and vibrates to its frequency or frequencies of similar form. This applies to all forms of energy, sound, vision, thought, colour and light. Take colour for instance, which is merely energy vibration at difference frequencies put into order by the perception of our minds. As well as being effected by other forms of energy they are also effected by attune thought, which vibrates to different frequencies. Even sound will vibrate to difference frequencies within itself depending on the pitch of the sound. If a sound gets too loud we will not hear it but our pet cat or dog will hear it until it goes beyond that pitch. Light also which is another of the forces that can be seen with the naked eye up to a point but when the vibration is raised it goes beyond infra red and ultra violet and beyond that into pure energy or light in the Divine scheme of things. In other words the higher the vibration of any force it changes or transcends into light. Even our very thought become light and we become one with it. We know we can exert physical change on a piece of metal through thought i.e. bending of spoons, a process called telekinesis, sometimes known as psychokinetic; the ability to influence energy / move objects by the power of the mind. We also know that we can heal others and ourselves by prayer or healing which is the intention of thought or collective thoughts (see chamber of healing).

So in the seventh vibration and to some extent in the fifth vibration in which the planet is now ascending to, we come to the awareness; that thought intellect is all-powerful and possible. Through creative visualization, imagination and meditation, a fusion of two or more forces of any of the forces can manifest in physical form.

Some readers may find this hard to grasp especially those still on the third vibration. , But as the vibrations of the planet shift this knowledge will no longer be esoteric or hidden but will be commonplace in homes, schools, hospital and workplaces. This is how things operate and manifest on the seventh vibration. Let me explain, In this chamber, scientists with their advanced intelligent minds using visualising techniques are able to create almost any monocles of any vibration, shape, form and texture, even so far as to the scent and smells of that which they create by the fusion of two or more atoms.

Everything that they create has not alone all the qualities of the single structure but also has become embedded in the creation of their thoughts and personalities at the time of creation. In this chamber nothing is made so to speak but is created by the power of intelligence minds. Nothing is created without a purpose and when it is no longer needed by anyone it dissolves again. Everything in the universe no matter how small or how great serves a purpose. This chamber is in charge of the new science, which thanks to Einstein and the like is evolving rapidly on the planet earth at present. You can see how things have shifted in modern western medicine in the last century and because of this shift, consciousness of east and west have come closer together. It would seem now that more and more people are getting together to hold the focus of love and light. Indeed they are networking together and finding a purpose for the common good. The Internet is one example, which is at present on earth facilitating chances in our thinking that the world is smaller than we think and that we are not separated, but united as a shared consciousness for the common good. This indeed is the actual teaching of this book. This will increase over the next hundred years or so. This united consciousness will bring religion, science, medicine and healing together and so help us to carry out our soul purpose, our soul purpose being something we love to do, even done for no fee. Money and the exchange of money will have no place in the seventh vibration as everyone works for the common good. Even today money is only recognised as a means of exchange as it is almost non-existent, electronically being exchanged from one country to another by computer keys. The days of the pounds shillings and pence have evolved to numbers and money certainly is not as tangible as it would have appeared in the physical world of our past. Money in the universal sense is purely energy in the form of notes and coins or bits of metal and paper with no value other that of our human perception in which it's held. Money is purely human constructed, the only reason money exists at all, is that we really believe that money is needed in order to manifest our desires. Of course this is not true. Long before money became a desire, our age old ancestors could manifest all their needs and desires because they realised that the universe was infinite with abundance and would provide them with everything they needed, not just money. Money has trapped so many in the third vibration and as long as we hold this belief that money is needed to manifest all our desires, we will remain a slave not just to money but to all material things. We will not move into the seventh vibration until there comes a shift in our belief system. Then we will understand the true meaning of money and will no longer be dependant on money. We will however still be able to manifest all we desire without focussing our need for money as a means of accomplishing those desires. This is the shift into the seventh vibration and a new consciousness of many new realities and possibilities in many fields not just money.

The science of the seventh vibration will be the science of the 21st century and beyond. Two generations from now our grandchildren will regard surgery and drug therapy as been archaic just as we now regard a doctor from the Middle Ages sawing off someone leg using no anaesthetic, or the act of blood letting to cure a fever as barbaric. This does seem very gruesome now for anyone, at the present time, to comprehend but at the time it was science at it best. Let's look at this now in greater detail in the next chapter the chamber of healing and guides,

Greetings.

Chapter 5

Chamber of Healing & Guides

Well after reading the last chapter I think it would be fair to say that we have certainly come along way in evolution since the Middle Ages in regards to many things and not just healing. This was a time when the fourth energy hadn't even yet reached the planet from the Chamber of Council. However, there were of course the few souls, which were called saints that had already emerged into the light vibrations of the seventh vibration, but those were few and far between. Indeed the Middle Ages is given here only as an example of a time in our evolutionary history which was very dark times indeed, much darker than the last century and in the scheme of things it was pretty dark. However, the old Master say's that to appreciate light we must experience the dark, but in this chamber where the angels and the archangels and the higher master and guide reside there is no dark. They assure us that darkness will never overcome light as the new shift in consciousness emerges on the planet. This is a place of love and light of the higher intelligences who work many miracles in our evolution with the many light workers that are at present very active on the planet. Never before in our evolutionary journey did the chamber of council send so many lightworkers in such great numbers to help this planet to evolve and emerge into the light of the seven vibrations. This is the chamber of guides and healing. We will discus now some of the different roles this chamber plays in the collective consciousness of our planet. The members of this chamber are continually sending out rays of light to the third dimension time frame, both, on the inner planes of the planet to clear away what is held in the collective dustbin of the emotional residue of humanity. At present the seventh ray of light is very active, which is the purple ray of purification and healing. Healing is finding a balance between the blue rays of the male energies and the pink rays of the female energies, hence the purple rays. These rays, are, encoded into our planet by St Gemenine and Merlin the magician, from the inner spheres, which work side by side with the many lightworkers that are present on our planet.

Oh, yes we have certainly come a long way since the Middle Ages, and east has surely come closer to west on these matters according to eastern thinking. However before we get into all of that, lets look back a little on the history of healing

The twentieth century has produced such changes and advances in medicine that it has changed the earth beyond all recognition.

In 1901 in the United Kingdom, the expectation of life at birth, which is a primary indicator of the effect of health care on life span, was 48 years for males and 51 years for females. By the 1980's life expectancy had reached 71 years for males and 77 years for females, and today, 80 is the new sixty. Other developed nations showed similar dramatic increases. In fact, the outlook has so altered, that with the exception of cancer and aids, the focus has become redirected to keeping people fit rather than keeping them alive. Improvements in communication between scientists throughout the world has aided these changes. Through publications and later electronic media, scientists exchanged ideas and reported on their efforts. No longer did individuals work in isolation as, teamwork was the normal situation. Medical education for physicians and other health care professionals has kept pace with advances in medicine, especially in the industrialized countries. Each country maintains its own requirements for medical standards, and boards of certification have created strict requirements that physicians must meet.

There is also emphasis on the need for practicing physicians to continue their education. There is a disparity of quality of medical services between the developed and developing countries. This is primarily a matter of money, and international organizations such the World Health Organization and United Nations International Children's Fund make substantial assistance available in this regard. The history of an institution that cares for the sick can be traced to the Middle Ages when monks set aside areas of their monasteries for this purpose. The modern general hospital is the current extension of this. Specialization has occurred in medicine to a high level, due to the expansion of knowledge both in depth and range, which encouraged the development of new forms of treatment. Precision in diagnosis has markedly improved with advances in the use of radiology, ultra-sound and other modern technology. The problem with this level of specialization is that it is expensive. Governments in developing countries normally find that it is more cost effective to provide people with more basic care. Alternative medical therapies which perhaps should be called complimentary therapy became accepted at the end of the twenty century; to the extent that disciplines such as chiropractics and acupuncture, which were not accepted and were describe as the occult in the west in times past, have now become almost mainstream. Many other forms of healing using light, sound, manipulation, and a variety of techniques are currently being practiced, very effectively. One of the primary attributes of this alternative form of therapy is that it is generally non invasive. The first rule of healing is to ease the pain, the second rule is to induce sleep and the third rule is to cause no harm.

Alternative therapy/ complimentary therapy is the practical application of another way of approaching healing, Qi gong being the most popular form of self-healing. Although, originally from China, has rapidly spread westerly in the last twenty years or so. Qi-Gong dates back to the Quing Dynasties of 960–1911 ad. It was used in connection with mysticism and many people shrugged it off as superstition, but with advances in modern science and physics over the past century, there has been a resurgence of interest in it. Qi-Gong has been researched in the light of modern science and many of the exercises, which did result from superstition, have been tested and discarded but others have been retained. So in China today, Qi-Gong clinics have been set up to study and teach Qi-Gong and treat diseases (see hospital in China)

Qi gong is a system of stationery and moving physical meditations to channel the life force or chi (see chi) of a person to any part of the body or mind to achieve almost any result you wish. It can be used to strengthen any organ or organ system of the body that may be deficient or weak and not functioning at one hundred percent capacity. It can also be used to raise the general energy of a person to relieve stress or to attune yourself to your surroundings and the world at large. Qi gong works on the simple principle that energy is needed to work any muscle in the body and that energy must come from the body's energy store house, a point the Chinese call the "dantien" and flow from that point to any muscle in use. It is this path, which it flows through from the dantien to the muscle in use that allows Qi gong to work in a predictable manner. So by putting the body in a certain physical position and adopting a relaxed mind state which the Chinese called "Saun" we cause the energy to flow through our energy pathways or meridians which relate to a particular part of the body we wish to energise and provide the environment conducive to it healing itself. It is this predictability that electricity has, that allows us to use it in our homes, hospitals and cars etc. To use electricity we merely create a pathway for it to travel along (a circuit) and then place a resistance of some description in the way. The electricity will operate the item in its way not because it wants to but because it wants to continue on its way and so by passing through the resistance i.e. light bulb, motor, blender etc it can continue on its way to the earth. As the predictability of electricity allows us to use it, the same is true of Qi gong. The body's energy patterns are predictable and by placing the diseased part of the body in the path the energy wishes to travel the energy will help to heal that part of the body. This is not because it wants to because energy has no consciousness and cannot make decisions, but because the law of physics dictates that it will continue to travel along that path and if it must pass through a diseased part of the body to do so then so be it. This of course is only a brief outline of the physical aspects of Qi gong and Qi gong physical healing; however at a more esoteric level the equivalent of physical healing is faith healing. Faith healing involves achieving recourse to Divine power to cure mental or physical disabilities, either with normal medical care, or in place of it. Often an intermediary is involved whose presence may be essential in effecting the cure. Sometimes the faith may reside in a particular location, which then becomes the focus of pilgrimage for sufferers. Faith in the healing power of natural springs is historic and widespread. In ancient Egypt and Greece, temples were erected near springs and festivals were held in honour of the Gods of the springs. In Christianity, faith healing is demonstrated in the miraculous cures brought about by Jesus and his Apostles. Forty healings are recorded in the Bible. The early church sanctioned faith healings through such practices as anointing with oil and laying on of hands. Faith healing has also been associated with the demonstration of miracles by Saints. An interesting extension of faith healings was the metaphysical healing movement in the United States called 'new thought'. This gave rise to the Christian Science movement, which published numerous articles telling their followers that there was a direct connection between the imminence of God and a link between bodily ills and mistaken convictions. Christian Science thought that sickness was subject to the powers of the individual spiritual being. Mary Baker Eddy founded Christian Science in 1879. It now has about 3,000 congregations in 56 countries. While the Christian Scientists do take advantage of some traditional medial services, they also use full time practitioners who are engaged in the healing ministry. They are usually paid a nominal amount by the Church and are paid by their patients. They are usually required to devote their full time to the healing work. Other such places is Dr Pang hospital / Centre in China .

The Center in China was established in 1988 in the city of Zigachong and later, in 1992, relocated to the city of Fengrun, two hours by train from Beijing. It is directed by its founder, Dr. Pang Ming, a Qigong grandmaster and physician trained in both Western and Chinese traditional medicine. This hospital is the largest of its kind in China.

The Centre avoids medicines and special diets in favour of exercise, love, and life energy. It is a non-profit organization and is recognized by the Chinese government as a legitimate clinic. Over the years, the Centre has treated more than one hundred and eighty diseases, the overall success rate being more than 95%. The method is based on the 5,000-year-old concept of qigong (chigong, chi kung) as well as modern medical knowledge. Dr. Pang, reverently known as Lao-shi, the Teacher, has written more than nine books on Chi-Lel.

Chi-Lel consists of four parts:

1. Strong belief (Shan Shin) - a belief that chi or life energy can heal all ailments, including one's own. Students build belief by listening to testimonials of recovered patients and learning about chi and its healing effects.

2. Group Healing (Chu Chong) - before a group of students begins Chi-Lel, the teacher verbally synchronizes the thinking of the group to obtain chi from the universe and bring it down into a healing energy field, shrouding everyone including the teacher himself or herself. The healing effect is enhanced because the group is acting as one.

3. Chi Healing (Fa Chi) - Facilitating chi healing by teachers - teachers bring healing energy from the universe to each individual to facilitate healing.

4. Practice (Lan Gong) - Students learn easy-to-follow Chi-Lel movements and practice them over and over again. The methods, parts of Zhineng qigong, are called 'Lift Chi Up and Pour Chi Down Method' and the 'Three Centers Merge Standing Method'. When a patient enters the hospital, he is diagnosed by a doctor and then assigned to a class of fifty or so people for a 24-day treatment period. He spends most of his time practicing Chi-Lel, eight hours a day without television, newspapers, or telephone. Those who can stand up practice standing up and those who can sit practice in their chairs; and those who can't move practice in their beds. Despite its amazing success at healing, the Centre is little known even in China because of its

policy of not advertising in newspapers or magazines. However, the Centre is well known among its estimated eight million Chi-Lel practitioners. Through word of mouth, thousands of people from all over China are coming to the Centre every month. Indeed, Chi-Lel has a great number of followers and the Center is the brain of this vast organization. New techniques for treating diseases are developed daily. For example, a new way of demonstrating the effectiveness of chi for treating cancer has been developed. The Centre has over six hundred staff members, including twenty-six Western-trained doctors. Since no medicine is prescribed, there aren't any pharmacists. Doctors, who prefer to be called teachers, play only a minor role in this special hospital. Occasionally, they are called upon to attend emergency cases. Their main function is to diagnose patients when they come in to register and again after each 24-day training period. Their diagnoses are classified into four categories for statistical purposes.

1. Cured: Symptoms disappear and appropriate instruments (e.g., EKG, ultra-sound, X-ray, CT and so on) register normal.

2. Very Effective: Symptoms almost disappear and instruments show great improvement.

3. Effective: Noticeable improvements and student can eat, sleep, and feel good.

4. Non-effective: No change or even worse.

According to A Summary of Zhineng Qigong's Healing Effects on Chronic Diseases, published by the Centre in 1991 data of 7,936 patients showed an overall effective healing rate of 94.96%. (15.20% cured; 37.68% very effective; 42.09% effective.) In the Centre, no matter how sick a person is, he/she is still addressed as a 'student' never 'patient' why? because he is learning an art, the goal of which is to heal oneself, not to rely on doctors. Therefore no doctor-patient relationships exist. A 24-day treatment program is only one hundred yuan (about twelve dollars). Students can spend as little as six hundred yuan (about seventy dollars) per month! The Center is probably the most inexpensive hospital in the world and is truly a non-profit organization. Yet the Centre is an independent, self-sufficient organization, without any help from government or private foundations.

How do they operate so efficiently? Because many of the doctors, Chi-Lel teachers, and supporting personnel are former students who have recovered from serious illnesses themselves and have now returned voluntarily to 'serve the sick' with very little pay. Teachers play the roles of doctor, nurse, social worker, cheerleader, parent, friend, brother, and sister. Their effectiveness is measured by the healing rates of their students.

Another reason for the Centre's effective but low-budget operation is that it uses group therapy. By living in groups, students develop in a cooperative spirit of caring and love toward each other. Many have been rejected by their former hospitals as 'incurable,' and, therefore, had regarded the Centre as their last hope. As though sailing on the same boat in the ocean, students bond together against their common enemy - disease. Just as hospitals associate with medical schools to train young people to enter into the medical profession, the Centre also has Chi-Lel schools to train Chi-Lel professionals. The Academy, established in 1992, has a two-year training program for young men and women under the age of thirty who have at least a high-school education. In addition, just as prestigious hospitals have research programs, the Center has many on-going research projects both on site and at different university campuses around the country. Besides doctors, teachers, and students, there are hundreds of supporting personnel, working in the office, cafeteria, bookstore, and so on. All of them are Chi-Lel practitioners and they practice Chi-Lel together in the morning and in the evening, about three hours a day. As they say, it is not just a job - it is a Chi-Lel job.

The Centre is open only ten months a year because of lack of heating in the rooms during winter. The Centre is currently building a home for itself - a "Chi-Lel City" in a place near Beijing, with better facilities to accommodate the ever-increasing number of students, including Americans and others coming from abroad. When the founder, Lao-shi, was asked why didn't he promote Chi-Lel to the world sooner? He replied "that many people need proof whether chi works or not". So instead of arguing with others, he preferred to work solidly by treating patients and collecting valuable data. As a result, tens of thousands of documented cases over a period of eight years have been collected and, now we are ready. Please tell the world that we exist and Chi-Lel can benefit mankind." Indeed it is time to tell the world that this centre exists and Chi-Lel can benefit mankind." This is the shift to the seventh vibration. Well done Lao-shi, (founder). At the beginning of the century the technological aspect of medicine has developed at an impressive rate. The next consideration must be the more holistic view of health in that a quality lifestyle is the key to all health and medical treatment, and as examples of the benefits of quality lifestyles are documented, others seeking sparkling health and extended longevity will no doubt reproduce them. Let's look at other aspects of healing and healers views of the past that had already evolved into the seventh vibration and indeed let's look at healing in the seventh vibration.

Here I would like to explain about the word Chi or Chi energy as it is so commonly known these days and also because I used the word quite a bit in the last few chapters, so bear with me. Chi is the intrinsic energy that sustains all life forms and substances in the universe. It is the life force that regulates the ebb and flow of the vitality of all things. It is referred to as prana in India, shanskrit or rlung in Tibetan and ki in Japanese. Aristotle referred to it as the soul of energy that exists in all nature where signs of life are to be found. Everything exists in this vast universal energy system i.e. the alpha and the omega; there is no beginning and no end. This continuous ebb and flow of energy is unfolding and changing and remains as perennial as the grasses. What is now always will be and is moving and evolving at a tremendous rate. We are only scraping the surface of this energy field in modern technology. Everything is evolving, including us humans, at a very fast rate, physically, mentally and spiritually. We really are truly remarkable and as there is nowhere in the body that does not require blood and nutrient to survive and function properly. Therefore, there is no part of the body that does not require energy to survive and function i.e.; every cell. Harry Edwards called this the body intelligence.

The first and probably the most important point here is that the bodies natural wish is to heal itself when given the correct environment. Look at it from a simple level for instance you cut your finger you may need to do no more than to clean the affected area and put a band-aid on the wound to cover it. If the wound is large it may require several stitches to mechanically bring the skin together, so the body repairs the damage. Even in regards to major microsurgery where a served limb is rejoined, the surgeon mechanically puts back in place the hand or foot and rejoins the blood vessels, nerve, fibres, skin etc. but the actually healing process is done by the body. This is however not to minimise the magnificent skills involved in performing such intricate tasks as microsurgery, but it is however I think putting things in their true perspective and recognising the body's true role in healing. It is only the body that heals, all the practitioner does, be they doctor or complementary therapist or spiritual healer, by the administration of drugs, herbs, massage, surgery Qi gong aromatherapy or whatever, is to provide the body with the necessary tools and the best possible environment to work with. This of course is borne out many times by people dying because they lost the will to live, or the reverse of people defying all odds and their doctor predictions and making miraculous recoveries from deaths door because of their immense will to live. I would like to continue to the second point I wish to make, and that is the mind body medicine. The point made above regarding the will to live, is a good example of this and the placebo effect, which is always taken into consideration when testing new drugs, medical therapies, or processes on people, is another. There are literally hundreds if not thousands of ways in which the body's ability to manufacture almost any chemical compound in response to a particular situation is used in medicine everyday. The most common one is immunisation whereby a minute dose of disease in which you want to guard against is give to the patient to get the body to manufacture the required chemical to protect the person against the disease.

So in the last chapter we have established that the body heals and that there is an organisational energy force directing the chemical and cellular healing process, which will eventually repair the damage. Harry Edwards called this organisational energy force the body intelligence, which he believed had to be directed by something beyond the mind and brain but for now, let's look at how the mind directs the energy, especially in self healing. If you are seated at a table, and in front of you is a bowl of fruit and if you think to yourself that you would like an apple, that thought is not physical. It is at first hand something that dwells purely in the mind. An abstract thing, it then becomes our electrical impulse in the brain, and eventually an energy level process. This electrical impulse sets in motion an amazing array of chemical actions and nerves responses, which enable you to lean forward, reach out and pick up the apple. A simple task that many do every day, but what has happened is that the mind, that abstract thought process, has created reality through electrical and then chemical actions. The use of the mind to direct the energy to cause electrical and chemical actions to take place is the basis for self-healing and indeed to some extent healing others. While doing Qi gong, given in the above chapter is only an example which involves placing the body in certain physical positions so that the energy system of the body is directed in certain ways to gain predictable results. These predictable results are gained because to move to any physical position or to maintain that position, requires, that certain energy pathways be activated or open, and by knowing which organ system or part of the body this relates to, you can direct the energy to whichever part of the body that you wish. However, it is not the object of this chapter to teach Qi gong which simply means working on the life force potential of a person or patient...(see Qi gong) but rather to present it as a viable opinion and complement to accepted western medical practice, and certainly in my opinion a way of awareness of self healing and healing others. Of course this is only on the surface, healing goes much deeper that this. Every healing has a purpose and the treatment must be a planned act. To carry out a planned treatment requires intelligence and direction. With the successful healing of a medically incurable disease, the intelligence must possess greater skills and wisdom than the earthly Doctors .If this intelligence is not of the third vibration it must certainly come from the intelligence of the seventh vibration. As there are Doctors on the earth third vibration, there are also Doctors or what are called spirit guide on the seventh vibration which have far greater wisdom and intelligence than of any mind from the third vibration could possible understand. In this chamber, Doctors are scientists and scientists are Doctors. They are all involved in healing and working with people on earth i.e. lightworkers that have shifted to the seventh vibration.In order for a new consciousness to emerge, the old school of thought needs to be stripped and destroyed in the purple rays of truth, which is the seventh energy of the planet. This is brought to earth through healers (lightworkers) and their awareness of collective consciousness with their spirit Doctors or guides. We will look at spirit guides later. This process is known as the seven years tribulation that so many have spoke about in the past, the period between 2005 and 2012. The seventh rays are an energy that comes to the planet every six months. This energy is filled with love, which will remove all fear of controlled empowerment that has griped humanity through the ages and to bring consciousness to a higher level rather that being over powered by outside influences. Now is the time for self-empowerment but I will explain in the last Chamber of Transition & Transformation, how this empowerment can and will be achieved as it is part of the Divine will, for now back to healing.

Let's look at healing of a arthritic joint, the joint can not move or only partially move because it has been cemented lock tight with arthritic deposits. This locking of the joint has constricted the ligaments and tendons and so therefore no amount of physical force can make the joint move freely while in this state. Because of the level of pain Doctors would have to give a patient an anaesthetic before attempting to move the effected joint. But this will not heal the arthritics, as the healing of arthritics can not be helped in any way by manipulation. First there must be a chemical change to remove the arthritis deposits. We know from the chamber of science, that all matter is composed of atoms and that each atom is a form of energy of different elements constructed in an identical way. We know to that when one form of element is associated with that of an another form of element it produces a third substance etc and this is how chemical changes are brought about. To bring about a change in any matter additional energies have to be applied to it just the same as to change water to steam we must bring the water to boiling point. In healing of an arthritic joint which can only take place within the seventh vibration it follows that some other substance has to be applied to the arthritic joint to induce a chemical change. In medical science this is the basis of clinical treatment of which deep ray therapy is an example. Arthritis is however medically incurable and medical science of the third vibration have not yet been able to discover any form of substance or force of energy to dissolve the crippling adhesions. We also learned from the chamber of science that sciences now of the third vibration are able to split the atom and release its power to create nuclear energy. Healers, science and Doctors who work together on the seventh vibration with the help of spirit Doctors or guides do the same thing but with much more advance knowledge and wisdom. (See chamber on wisdom and knowledge).

I think now at this stage of the book which I hope you are enjoying so far, it would be only fair for you the reader to look more closely at spirit doctors or spirit guides. Spirit guides is the more common name used these days, as more and more people make the shift in collective coconsciousness.

Spirit Guides

Spirit Guides are entities or beings that are currently in the spirit realms or dimensions. These are individuals, or groups of individuals, who have agreed with a person on the earth plane to act as their guide or guardian. Usually we enter into this agreement with at least one "primary guide" prior to being born into a physical body. These "primary guides" are often other members of our Soul Group, and we have quite likely traded "guide duties" with them during various lifetimes. (That's a generalization, of course; however there are undoubtedly a frequent number of exceptions.) We can also call other guides to us as we need or desire their extra help, and it is not uncommon to have two or more guides assisting us at a given moment. Many of the guides with whom we work are beings who have lived on this earth plane at one time or another (or many lifetimes), but there are guides who are from other worlds as well. Also, many of the "special guides" who come to help us with special needs or learning experiences seem to be more evolved beings, or 'old souls' who willingly share their expertise and expanded knowledge with those of us still working on our evolvement and enlightenment. Guides, while similar to Angels, are somewhat different, but their "duties" or influences can overlap each other. Many people believe that Spirit Guides and Angels are one and the same thing, and that's fine too. Angels, though, seem to be on a slightly different plane, and seem to have a slightly different purpose for working with humans. Angels, especially Guardian Angels are more the type to hover nearby and assist in emergencies even without our asking them to. While Spirit Guides, although they will help unasked, are more our teachers and guides rather than specifically guardians One of the "separations" is that Angels are working on a little different "plan of evolvement" than Spirit Guides. While Spirit Guides are often beings who have lived on this earth plane themselves, Angels are beings who have worked through their evolvement elsewhere and are now serving as Guardians and 'inspirers' for those of us evolving here. However, I am aware that in some instances, it does seem that some humans achieve 'angel status' upon their passing over into the next dimension, and then work from that perspective. And, of course, we do know that Angels can and do appear in 'human form' from time to time, just as Spirit Guides can and will show themselves in a 'physical manifestation.' But this takes a lot of energy and seldom happens.

One of the primary purposes that Spirit Guides have is the guiding and teaching of those under their care. They agree to help us remember the lessons we set up for ourselves in this life, and to instruct us with regards to those lessons. They can, and will, teach us as much as we want to learn and their guidance is of a very gentle nature. They will not give us any more information than we are ready to receive and capable of perceiving. They're here to help us to learn, but they won't shove the information on us if we decide we really don't want to do that work i.e. healing. In other words they won't write the messages in the sky for us.

They'll counsel and help us see other perspectives, but they won't make the decisions for us; the choices are always ours to make and to live with that decision afterwards. We usually have one or two "primary" Spirit Guides. These are the ones that we make the arrangements with before being born, to guide us and help us learn the lessons we set up for ourselves. They gently remind us when we're a bit "off path" from our original plans for this lifetime. But we actually have an unlimited number of Spirit Guides available to us. We can call "special guides" to teach us specific lessons, and once those lessons have been learned, they will move on to help others. Also, as loved ones pass over, they can choose to act as additional Spirit Guides for us either 'full time' or on an 'as needed' basis. While we usually keep the same "primary" Spirit Guides, the rest of our guides can often vary and fluctuate. As I said before, we call to us those guides we need at a specific time for a specific purpose. Also, if we have loved ones who are acting as some of our guides, they will also have work of their own to do in the other dimensions. Their lives are as real to them now as they were when they were in the physical world and as real to them as our lives are to us. The only difference is that our lives are material and physical while their lives are esoteric and spiritual.

Hence they will go about their work, and be "a little removed from us" for periods of time. But they can, and do, hear us when we call, and return to assist us in whatever way they can. They communicated telepathically with us (see telepathy). There are many ways to contact Spirit Guides! One way, is through meditation. Meditating and asking for communication with your guides, and then listening for their response, is a really good way. Guided Meditations aimed specifically at meeting a guide can be very useful. Dreams are another way. Often if we are too busy living, and we don't remember to meditate and listen, then our night dreams become the only time we're quiet enough to receive their messages. Automatic Writing is another interesting way of receiving direct communication from guides. When you combine Automatic Writing with meditation, it frees your mind to allow the incoming messages to be recorded. These are only three of the many ways in which to receive guidance from your Spirit Guides. By the way, synchronicity can often be an indication that you've got a Spirit Guide trying to get your attention!

There are many ways that Spirit Guides will alert a person to their presence. In other words, many things can let us know that we've got a guide around us. One that jumps instantly to my mind is the use of fragrances. Many guides and spirit entities use scents and odours to signal they are there. If this happens, you'll get a whiff of some fragrance that has no "physical source" or explanation. It can be any kind of scent: sweet, sour, pungent, floral, obnoxious, etc, but usually sweet smelling especially the guides from higher realms will manifest themselves with a sweet smelling scent hence the scent of roses that many lightworkers are experiencing at present on the planet. Sometimes the guide will just use something that is unique, or maybe something familiar from one of his or her own past lives. Other times they will use a fragrance that has specific connotations or memories for you! One set of "temporary guides" that spent some time with me used the scent of roses that I couldn't identify. I later found out, with the help of a friend, that this was a fragrance of Divine Intervention and many people associate with saints which holy people of the past but today is quite popular on the planet and many like-minded people are experiencing it. Sounds are another way. Some guides and entities will use auditory signals such as the sound of "chimes" that you seem to hear. In some cases the sound will be audible to anyone in the vicinity; sometimes only you will hear it. There are many other ways including chills, goose bumps, and "energy brushes." Synchronicity is also a sure sign, in my book, that guides and/or angels are trying to get our attention! To borrow a phrase: Spirit energy seems to move in mysterious ways. So never discount any possibilities. While most of the time, when you're communicating with your Spirit Guides, you're relatively "closed" to any other contact; there is the potential of "inviting in" other entities. Especially under some circumstances like Automatic writing which needs to be done under total mind control. But if you take some basic precautions, you need never encounter or experience negativity or negative beings. Whenever you sit down to meditate, or do Automatic Writing, or in any way try to contact your guides, take a few seconds to do a "protection" for yourself and your surroundings. There are several ways of doing this, and all will work and are "good." Basically, any prayer or spoken 'intent' that you will invite only "beings of light" to enter the area and communicate with you is effective. Here's one that I use: While visualizing this you can say, either in your mind or aloud a protective chant like:

"I call on all the positive powers of the universe, my guides and masters, to assist me in my mission and be a channel for the light".

You have to ask your Spirit Guides for their assistance! This is one of the very subtle ways in which Angels and Spirit Guides differ from each other, I think. Angels, especially Guardian Angels, are much more apt to help without being asked, or so it seems. While Spirit Guides will help up to a point without being asked, certain "laws" bind them from interfering with our lives. Before we were born, we set down certain lessons and experiences for ourselves in this lifetime. Our guides will help to set these things up for us, but they do truly need for us to ask them to help us in more specific ways. There's a little thing called "free will" at work here which says that we have the right to do as we please even to the point of ignoring the lessons we originally set up for ourselves. And our guides, and most of the angels, cannot interfere with our freedom to choose. It's a very fine line, between helping us and interfering with our "free will " and one they have to walk very carefully. So do we have to ask our Spirit Guides for their help? Yes and No. They will help unasked to a certain extent, and try to get our attention if we're not tuning into them. That's part of the reason they agreed to be our guides, but I do believe that beyond that point, we do have to ask! If we want the wonderful teachings they have to offer us, we have to ask for it, and then listen! If we want the extra boost over a particularly rough spot, we have to ask. The "bottom line" is that our guides are willing to help in any way they can, but we have to live our own lives and they cannot interfere with the living of our lives as the choice is ours. I'm finding in my own life that one of the really "key" points in working with my guides seems to be 'asking questions.' If I just meditate, and listen, I'll probably hear a little bit more and at the very least feel a presence. But it's only that I remember to ask questions -- and the more specific the question seems to be, the better, which I begin to get strong answers and more insights. The challenge is of course figuring out which questions to ask, as my mind is very active and to be patient and wait for an answer.

"I've been led to understand that our Guides will endeavour to help us whenever they can, but will stop short of "living our lives for us" (unless asked to do so). No, I don't mean they'll take over our life for us if we ask them to, but rather they cannot interfere with our "free will" (except in cases of dire emergency). They prefer the role of "helper" to the role of "ruler." If we invite them to help, they will but if we don't, they're limited in the kinds of help they can offer without violating our right to free will, not helping without an invitation. In my own experience there seems to be messages coming all the time especially in dreams and meditation, that does tell me it's time to ask for help before I jump in headfirst and make trouble for myself. However very often I get messages that say I'm doing okay." While I know the identity of several of my guides, I do not know who all of them are. Some have given me names while others choose not to. This seems to be pretty much "standard" for Spirit Guides from what I've read. Some have no problem with giving you a name to identify them by and some will give you a symbol to use as a name. Some feel that we will be distracted by names and identities. Seeing Spirit Guides is very much like all the other psychic-related things and not that important. What's important is that we believe in ourselves. Some see their guides and some don't and some see them part of the time. I suspect the majority of us, though, don't actually see our guides. We can and do, however, sense them on many levels. Personally, I haven't been able to open up too much to psychic vision (or physical manifestation of a guide), yet, so I haven't seen my guides for the most part, at least not on physical manifestation but certainly I felt their energy and presence about. Indeed many a times I would get mental pictures of my guides relayed to me and indeed other healers and mediums who could see them through their gift of clairvoyance, would describe them to me in the form of physical male or female manifestations or the manifestation of animals or birds i.e. black panther or the phoenix. There are many mythological explanations of the phoenix in many cultures Japanese, Egyptian, Arabian, and Chinese however I prefer the Chinese (Feng Huang) explanation, (see below).

In Chinese mythology the phoenix is a symbol of great virtue, grace, power and prosperity. It represents the unity of yin and yang. It was thought to be a very gentle creature and it is said that in China only an Emperor could wear the phoenix symbol on his tunic. It is said that the phoenix represents great powers sent from the heavens to the Empress. Sometimes a phoenix was used to decorate a person's house and that being the case, that person was of high virtues, loyalty, honesty, decorum and justice. So now back to the guides.

There are other ways of being aware that our guides are around. Many of the guides will "signal" you of their presence with auditory sounds or as I have already said by a scent of roses. Several of my guides have chosen these methods of letting me know when they're nearby. Some guides or angels will put a feather in your path to make you realise that they are around and are here to help you .The finding of feathers is a sign from the angels that it's your time to step up to the plate; so to speak. It is time to accept your soul mission to trust and not be afraid to follow that mission through.

Apparently the "standard" form of most spirits in the next dimensions is basically an energy form. And while all spirits seem to have unique energy forms, -- at least they can tell each other apart, whereas we might not be able to do so. The thing is however, that they also have the capability of "moulding" their energy into form and appearance of any and all of their incarnations on the earth's physical plane. So, if they show themselves to us, or we are able to see them by some manner (physically, etc.), then it is most common to see them in the form/incarnation that we will most likely recognize. For instance, if a grandmother has passed over and then reappears to us, she's going to look pretty much like we remember her or in a photograph. The exception to this is that they do seem to favour the appearance where they looked the best. In other words, if they were 70 when they passed over, and maybe not in the best of health, it's likely that they will choose to use the form of how they looked at age 40 or 50. In the case of a guide we've not met or been acquainted with in this lifetime, if it's a deceased loved one that some other family member will recognize, the same still holds true. However, if no one now would "recognize" the person, then they will usually use the form from a lifetime that was especially important, memorable, or significant to them in their own soul growth. (This all holds true with any spirit contact such as my healing sessions, "random visits" from deceased loved ones, dream visits, etc.)

How to work with your guides

Write down your question(s) if you wish or plant them firmly in your mind. Sit or lie in a comfortable position where you will not be disturbed breath normal, ground and centre yourself by remaining calm and relaxed. Become aware of each breath you take, however focus only on your breathing for a short time, as too much concentration on your breath can only distract you. Picture a landscape that is comfortable to you: a cave, a beach, a meadow, a forest clearing. Wherever your mind takes you is where you are supposed to meet your guardian. Not only see this landscape, but concentrate on the smells and the sounds around you. Continue visualizing your surroundings until they are firmly planted in your mind and you can see, smell and hear clearly everything that is around you. This may take some practice, and you may wish to work only up to this point until you can become immersed in this world. This is the reality of the seventh vibration. Picture a well or running water in the middle of this landscape. Imagine all of your negative feelings being bundled into a black ball in the middle of your body. Push this black ball outside of yourself and throw it into the moving water or well and see it leaving you. Now picture a white ball of light hovering over your head. See this white light descend and spread over your body until it fills you with white light. Call upon your guardian or spirit guide to be with you. You do not have to talk out loud. You will know when your guide is present - it may appear to you physically or you may hear voices in your head, you may smell flowers or perfume of some sort or you may simply feel a tingling sensation, especially on the back of your neck or sometimes a strong ringing in your ear. Keep calm and greet your guide and ask your question(s) or simply converse with it. You may get an answer right away - it could be spoken, it could be a symbol of some type. You may not receive your answer until later, even days later, so after your exercise be very aware of patterns or symbols you come across in your everyday life. Remember there are no such thing as coincidence's.

When you are finished conversing, thank your guide or angel. Return to normal consciousness by becoming aware again of your breathing and the sounds around you, ground and centre again, have fun.

Greetings.

Chapter 6

Chamber of Crystal

Crystals have been used by ancient healers, mediums and meditation masters for centuries and are just now being rediscovered on earth once again. Thankfully there are those people who have always held high regard for crystals and their healing properties. However, there are still some people who think that crystals have very little power. They believe that crystals have amplifying, absorbing properties or functions for the advanced healer and mediums. Their beliefs are that Crystals are only tools that extend the power of intent of the healer and a medium. This would be true of one's awareness in the third vibration but not in the fifth or seventh vibration. But as I said in my early messages on the seventh vibration; Crystal is everywhere and in everything including cloths, furniture, buildings, jewellery from the binding of books to household utensils everything and has indeed great healing properties

I am sharing this knowledge to those interested in crystals beyond their aesthetic appeal and glamour because of their necessary value for mastery in healing and spiritual ascension. Crystals are Earth's gifts to humans. They are living energy and in a way they are the keys to the Universe for healing, spiritual growth and ascension. Each particular type of crystal or mineral can be seen as a key, and we can use these keys to access specific energies, whether that is for healing, meditation, protection or understanding, as well as a thousand other uses. Crystals have been mined and used for thousand of years, and can be seen in ancient crowns, regalia and jewellery. Lapis Lazuli was ground up into paint and was used to decorate temples and icons.

Crystals Have Their Own Energy

Crystals can enhance, promote and help bring in chosen energies, for instance Tourmaline's help at times of change, within the tourmaline family there are different types such as black for deflecting negativity, green for emotional and watermelon (pink and green), and red for all help during times of change although in different ways. Topaz brings clarity and higher perspectives, blue for emotional, gold for creativity. Diamond is an amplifier and purifier, Ruby strengthens the will and gives courage and Emeralds helps to turn negativity into positivity. Crystals have their own frequency/energy. Rose Quartz is a specific nurturing energy i.e. a mother/love stone. When you feel down, you hold a cleansed Rose Quartz you will begin to harmonise with the frequency of the Crystal, and absorb the feelings (frequency) of love and care into your aura. It is the heart feminine stone but it also works well for males too, increasing their motherly love and bringing out their feminine side. There are no hard-hearted mortals on the seventh vibration but there are the warriors. A warrior is someone who has evolved through the many trials and tribulations of many life times in many existences. A warrior is someone who can kill as well as heal because in order to heal with compassion many had to kill first. Many warriors are known on earth from ancient times but many now have chosen to be reincarnated to heal again and to teach some of the wise old wisdoms to the people on earth, as they know from past experience that killing is not the answer and that two wrongs don't make a right. If you live by the sword you die by the sword, (see chamber of connection). Now, back to Crystals.

How Do Crystals Affect Us

Well we all have our own life/energy force, and we have energy portholes or vortex called Chakras (see Chakras). We have seven major Chakras, each with a specific function. When we're tired, stressed, unwell or depressed our Chakras can slow down or even stop working (which really isn't that uncommon in the stressful society that we are part of). Healers use Crystals in their practice to realign Chakra. They can assist the healing process, and can be programmed for particular jobs such as, cleansing etc. Crystals have a close affinity to our body elementals and to the earth, which build the energy of our base Chakra. At the base of the spine most people have depleted due to inherent weakness, stress low immune system defences, negative thought forms and emotions, and drug addiction. Because of the Crystals affinity to earth, it grounds a person's kidney energy through their feet up to their base Chakra. The Crystal has great properties when used for healing and mediumship by a healer. It really helps to keep them grounded and amplifies the whole healing process. Indeed Crystals hold the key to unlocking a vast new technology based upon the manipulation of etheric energies for healing as well as other applications. Because of their special geometric patterning, crystals are able to tap into universal energy patterns and frequencies that science is only beginning to discover. What scientists have not yet realized is that the ordered patterns of crystals, and their relationship to etheric fields, are similar to the ordered molecular structure of permanent magnets and their associated magnetic fields.

Choosing the Right Crystal for You:

The best way is to let your intuition guide you. If you feel really drawn to one piece that's the one for you. It can be incorporated into jewellery or be raw pieces. Crystals in their natural form are the most powerful. When crystals are cut, shaped and polished they can lose their natural force. However if the piece you like has been shaped and polished working and wearing the stone will bring energy and life back to the stone and it will perform its natural function.

Cleaning Crystals

When you buy a crystal, one of the first things you need to do is clean it. An ideal way is to place the crystal under the cold tap and turn the water on so it flows over the stone/s and down the plughole, this will take out the impurities and leave the stone clean and revitalised. Another way is to leave it on a sunny windowsill and let the sunlight cleanse it. A good way of checking the stone is to dowse it, hold the dowser/pendulum over the Crystal and see what happens. The pendulum should pick up a clockwise swing, if the Crystal is dirty then it could be a slow or a small swing. Cleanse the stone and check again. There should be a noticeable difference in the energy of the stone. Sometimes indeed crystals that are not cleansed will upset the energy of trained healer and medium

In the seventh vibration crystal is everywhere and in everything such as clothes, furniture, building, jewellery, binding of books and households utensils and has great healing properties. The main properties of Crystals are their healing properties. Crystals have a unique energy that reflects on earth as the seven colours of the rainbow, a sort of a magical power that vibrates at a very high frequency and that stimulates and penetrates the Chakra system of the human body. You can see it's wonderful effects and colours when you hold it against the sunlight and if you use sunlight and Crystals together on earth they will have immense healing abilities. As many lightworkers know by now, bringing in the sunlight to the third eye by the practise of sun gazing is becoming quite popular at present and is spreading across the globe. This practice though according to many is somewhat weird, but to the new age science of the seventh vibration, this practice will give a new direction to humankind and solve many of the ills of present day human society. This simple practice will give solutions on all fronts in relation to physical, emotional, mental and spiritual diseases. As a matter of fact, it is the rebirth of a science practiced in ancient times throughout, so nothing knew here.

Many spiritual writings and teachings that I have studied over the years are reviving and regenerating this lost practice

In different parts of India it is known as Surya / Namaskar or Sun Salutations. A similar practice was in Greece, and in Egypt it was called Heliotherapy, and so to in the Americas – Brazil, Mexico, Peru. The Inca civilization, which spread over South and North America, practiced it. INCA means sun. An example is the health resort sun temples of Machu Pichu, Peru.

Ancient writings found on these mountaintops describe how to gather energy through the sun. Energy from the sun has been used since times immemorial. We know it is a scientific fact that without sun or its energy nothing will survive, every creature and all energies electrical, magnetic, wind directly or indirectly sources itself in from the sun.

Today we rarely use the sun energy willingly as we are scared of the solar radiation and treat it like the enemy. Many human crises occur due to the lack of sun energy. The first major crisis is mental tension and worries, which leads to no self-confidence, negative thinking, fear, anger, irritation, greed, hostility, and lack of compassion. All these are ailments of the mind. The biggest setback we have is we suffer from poor immunity. We have no energy to tackle day-to-day living.

However many people in the world today say that we can overcome all this by taking sun energy. It is an established fact that total health includes mental, physical and spiritual wellness.

We have a super computer in our bodies given to us by nature. This is our brain. The brain is more powerful than the most advanced super computer. Each and every human being is gifted with innumerable talents and infinite inherent powers by nature. Individuals should never underestimate themselves. Everyone is gifted and all gifts are special. If we make use of these powers we can take ourselves to great levels. Unfortunately these infinite inherent powers are programmed in that part of the brain that is largely dormant and goes unused. Even medical science agrees that we only make use of about 5-to7% of the brain and even one of the the most brilliant of humans

Albert Einstein is reported to have used only about 32% of his brain.

Sun energy is the source that powers the brain. Sun energy can enter and leave the human body or the brain only through one organ and that is the human eye. The eye is the Sun Energy's entry door to the human brain, hence why the eyes are also known as the window of the soul (see energy projection). The eyes are a delicate part of the body. We have to use them in such a way that their purposes are served and they don't get damaged.

There are definite foolproof ways of getting from nature the benefits it has to offer and not exposing ourselves to its adverse affect. Present day teachings and ideas tell us not to look at the sunlight at all or you will damage your eyesight and never to go out in the sun as you will get cancer. This is causing needless hysteria and paranoia. The more you are away from nature the more there is cause for illness.

A lot of people have remained in good health just on sun energy historically. Accordingly in 1922 the Imperial Medical College in London decreed that solar rays are the ideal food for humans. But no one has mentioned what his or her technique is. A common reply was that the sun energy is entering through a secret door and reaching the medulla oblongata in the brain. They did not divulge their secret. This knowledge was lost to common folk. But like everything in today's world, through mass media and the Internet, this knowledge is no longer hidden and as I have mentioned earlier many spiritual teachings are reviving this practice.

This can be accomplished at any time of the year by anyone in any part of the World. In Brazil, Australia, Germany more than 3000 people are doing this practice. These People are feeling and looking much younger with less and less requirements for sleep, or material things and less and less food requirements. Indeed there are thousands of people around the globe and food has bid goodbye to them.

It is not that they have stopped eating. It is just that they don't feel hungry.

This I know sounds crazy to the reader and perhaps at this point you would feel like turning the page, but I as I said there's nothing knew about all of this. In fact in ancient times, this was a spiritual practice and now it is a scientific practice. It can be followed by anyone. When the results become reproducible it will become scientific. This practice will create a stir and will become a challenge to conventional medicine. But I'm not writing this to create a stir. My intentions are admirable, and they are to pass on this ancient wisdom so that we all can become truly independent. We all love to be independent. But are we independent? We become independent if we solve our own mental, physical, and spiritual problems. Easier said than done one might say. Well enough said. Let's look at how to practice and who knows the results you will achieve, but you must practice.

As we make use of the sun's power supply and we make use of the energized brain it becomes less and less dormant.

To determine when the sunrise is or the sunset period check the local newspaper to get the daily timings. Both times are good for practice and it depends on the individual.

Sun gazing is a one-time practice of your lifetime. Look at the rising or setting sun, one time per day.

Receive sunlight only in the morning or evening hours 1 hour after sunrise or 1 hour before sunset. It is proven beyond a reasonable doubt that at these times one is free from UV and IR rays' exposure. The UV index remains at 2 all through out winter. The best times to take a sunbath other than winter times are the 2-hour before sunset or 2 hour after sunrise. Gazing has the added advantage that you get vitamin A and D 1 hour before sunset or 1 hour after sunset. Vitamin A is necessary for the health of the eye and the only vitamin that the eye requires. It is safe to gaze during the one-hour period of sunrise and sunset or during winter when the intensity is less. .

First day look for a maximum of 10 seconds. On the second day look for 20 seconds at the rising sun and adding 10 seconds every succeeding day. So at the end of 10 continuous days of sun gazing you will be looking at the sun for 100 seconds i.e. 1 minute and 40 seconds. Stand on the earth with bare feet. Eyes can blink or flicker. Stillness or steadiness of the eyes is not required. Why don't you watch the sun instead of the TV? The intensity of the TV is much more than the rising or setting sun. If you can watch TV you can easily watch the rising or setting sun safely. Have a belief component in you that the sun rays or light that you are getting into the eyes is of immense benefit and will not harm you.

This will give you earlier, quicker and better results. Without fail, even without a belief component, you will get results if you follow the practice but it will take longer time, that's all.

You need not restrict any of your normal daily routines in life. There are no restrictions. No fasting, enjoy your food. It is a hunger that will disappear, food that will leave you. Fasting will happen. Consider gazing from the same place at the same time daily and will have its advantages. Adding sun gazing to your daily routine will not disturb the flow of the daily routine. If you pray, you can have any prayer of your choice. Any prayer, no particular one is suggested and prayer is not a requirement. As a precaution have your eyes examined by your doctor. This is to be on the safer side from the scientific viewpoint. If your cheeks get heated up then stop gazing. Use common sense.

When you reach 3 months you would have gazed at the sun 15 minutes at a stretch. When you can watch TV for 3 hours, surely you can see the sun for that long? What is happening as you go up to 15 minutes? The sun energy or the sunrays passing through the human eye are charging the pathway behind the retina leading to the human brain. As the brain receives the power supply through this pathway it activates our inherent brain's software programs have to start running. We realize we are a different person now. No mental tension or worries. We have the self-confidence to face life problems. We no more think negatively and only positive thoughts arise. All this is within 3 months. The first power has awakened. We humans have good and bad qualities and when sunlight enters the brain --good qualities come to the surface and replace bad ones.

Bad qualities disappear. Anger, greed and jealousy leave you. You become a lovable creature and a compassionate person.

Mental depression will go away. Psychiatrists are observing that SAD is caused by lack of sunlight. With the practice of sun gazing – you will not have depression in your whole lifetime. We will achieve a perfect balance of mind. Our biggest human crisis is over thinking. Sunlight definitely removes your mental diseases, food and sleep requirements decrease. Within 30 minutes duration of continuously looking at sun you will slowly be physically healthier, since by now all the colours of the sun reach the brain through the eye. Brain regulates the flow of colour prana appropriately to the respective organs. All the internal organs get ample supply of the required color prana or Chi. The vital organs are dependent on certain sun color prana-Kidney red, Heart yellow, Liver green etc. This is a well known fact in colour therapy

Within 6 months of sun gazing, this is when food intake decreases. No one needs to eat more than his or her hunger levels. Hunger comes because of energy requirements. The body requires energy and energy is a must. But eating too much food is not a necessity for the body to function. Only energy is. Conventionally we are indirectly getting sun energy while eating food which is a byproduct of sun energy. No sunlight means no food will grow. What we eat is secondary sun energy. In 6-9 months time we are starting to eat less and less.

Nearly all aroma, cravings, and hunger pangs disappear. However energy levels are high. In fact you will notice a gain in overall health, increase in energy and efficiency, decrease in sleep requirements while sleep quality increases; decrease in hunger and food intake; increased capacity to handle stress and be relaxed; increased ability to enjoy peace of mind and relationships with others and improved self-confidence, self-esteem and overall quality of life. These are the first noticeable advantages of practicing sun gazing.

We have to give up sun gazing now. Solar science prohibits further gazing after 9 months or 44 minutes for the sake of eye care. The body will get discharged when we stop sun gazing so we have to recharge, we do this by walking barefoot on the bare earth for 45 minutes daily, relaxed walking only. No need to walk briskly, jog or run. Any convenient time of the day preferably when the earth is warmer and sunlight is falling on your body.

When you walk barefoot an important gland in the brain's center called the pineal gland or the third eye is activated. The big toe of the foot represents this gland. 25 years ago it was considered a useless gland. Now it has become an important gland for study and about 18,000 papers have been published in the recent times.

It has always been known as the Seat of the soul. The Pineal gland has optic nerve endings. The remaining four toes represent glands too. When you walk barefoot, your body weight stimulates all these glands. This is strengthened by the earth heat/energy and the sun prana / chi falling on the head or the Crown Chakra. The Chakras are like doorways that take in the cosmic sun energies, they create a magnetic field and the body/brain recharges with the energy of the sun entering into it. Relax. Walk 45 minutes for one year. After one year of recharging, if you are satisfied with your progress you can give up barefoot walking. A few minutes of sun energy falling on you once in 3-4 days is enough now. However I still like to do my Qi gong's in the bare feet as it strengthens my immune system, memory power and concentration. As you increase the sun's heat on your feet the brain will activate the Pineal gland more and more.

This has enormous healing benefits especially on mental sickness. In fact the only thing you on earth have left from days gone by of sun worshipping is Sunday. The golden essences Divine energy is harness and in the sun light and no matter what history of the past has told you about the damage of sunlight to the body it's not quite true. Of course this is a two sided coin. Certainly too much of anything is damaging to the body but we are made to believe that staying out in the sunlight is harmful. In fact for centuries they have tried to keep this angelic energy away from us by building places of worship with little small windows, with little or no light getting in. We have been taken away from worshiping outside in nature and natural light in the last centuries and with the result we have not evolved a great deal in the last few thousands years, until now. Of course all of this was planned, as if the third eye was kept open. Being human and not yet having the experience of lives lived we would run out of control and probably end up zombies. So you see there had to be a balance between spirit and human or between, if you like, the Snake and the Angel, which is another book I am working on. Some say that the only thing we have left of the snake is our spinal column, DNA code and of course the reptilian brain. This would be correct but the snake represents the darker side to us, the power of intent, natural light and of course the connection to the earth .The snake knows that without this natural light it will not survive and it also knows that without the power of intent it will go hungry. On the other hand the Angel is pure light, love, and compassion and he/she realise that without love and compassion nothing can evolve. So it's the fuseing of these energies that makes us, if you like, a true energetic spiritual human being. So you see Crystal has both energies. Let me explain. Crystal come from rock from the ground i.e. from the earth but once it is fused with sunlight. It becomes vibrant colourful and emanates a vibration that transcends all dimensions. Put Crystal in sunlight in water first to cleanse it and see the many colours of the rainbow that are in it representing the seventh vibration, the angelic kingdom and the seventh Chakras as we understand it. Crystal has been used for millennium for many healing properties. What you see now happening on the planet is not something new but is age old wisdom of healing and science from ancient times of Atlantis, Arcturus and other worlds. These are all parallel worlds as you have seen from the chamber of wisdom and understanding. So as the vibration of the planet earth shifts a little more which it will do anyway with or without our help but better with the help of collective consciousness from the many light workers of travellers in time as these people will keep this planet from self destruction. So what Crystals will do for us in future is what food has done for us for a long time but as we advance into the next period in evolution our DNA strands of 2 will be activated to 12 strands. The snake will indeed unite with the angel and Crystallite chambers will be the new hospitals of the future. I stress the importance of crystal-light sunlight meditation. This form of healing is, as I said, an old age science of Atlantis time and which we on earth have been waiting for a long time. The way of the cross is definitely no longer necessary and the age old way of suffering and sickness will go forever but I said this would only happen with collected consciousness (see chamber of wisdom). Even at the time of writing this, humans are getting back to light as more and more buildings are designed to cater for more light, in all areas of our life, schools, hospitals, homes and workplaces. I said in my last book “A Way To Healing” that there was no such thing as darkness, only the absence of light. This is very true and as people open up more their physic qualities and let in more light through the heart Chakra, the planet and all on it will emerge in light. In fact the day of machines is coming to a close. As we are aware the oil is running out. Machines, though most of the time have done a good job, but again being human we took the negative approach and stayed in the darkness of our ignorance causing much pain and suffering. However, these were lessons we had to learn as we here on earth will be an example to other worlds of similar vibration, as we are one in a million that the Chamber of Council has chosen for this transition. We are one of the lowest forms of life on the universe but not the lowest. Just the same as your country Ireland was quite negative and trapped in superstitions and religious beliefs in ignorance of the past. It was by no means the worst. As time moves on your country will be an example to the rest of the world as many lightworkers have chosen Ireland and the British Isles to work from. As the vibrations shift and governments will trust one another instead of been suspicious as they were for centuries. Where Empires rose and fell worlds, governments today will start to come to together in a collective consciousness (see Christ consciousness) way of thinking. This will take some time but this will be the correct way forward. So machines will not be necessary as everything will evolve through light and this light will be stored and regenerated in what we call Crystal. Those of you who at present are studying Crystals I salute you.

Those of you who doubt the power of Crystal get a piece and place, it near you meditate in sunrise or sunset as the ultra violet rays are weaker at these times and see for yourself. Crystal has the power to transcend all vibrations and has the power to transcend all beliefs. It has in other words the power to energise your beliefs, thoughts, prayers etc. Some people might argue the old school of thought here and say that they have been praying for ages with little or no results. Look at the old Masters at how they pray. Give thanks first, this means give thanks for what you are about to receive, knowing and believing that you have already received it. Believe it, it will happen (see chamber of connection) As mentioned in the introduction; in the seventh vibration, Crystal will be everywhere in everything from cloths, to furniture, jewellery, buildings, from the binding of books to household utensils everything and anything and has great healing properties. But people this time round will not make a god of it or of its powers. Many of us have heard the saying, that money is the root of all evil. Really this statement is not true as money is not the root of all evil, but the enslavement of money is. This enslavement of money and material wealth is totally destructive to human evolution, but this will not happen with Crystal, as Crystal can be regenerated; how wonderful is that.

Greetings

Chapter 7

Chamber of Art & Fantasy

A fantasy is something you have projected; a dream is something that is not in existence as such, but which you have come to know.

There are no limits in the seven vibrations as we have the chamber of fantasy in which you can carry out any fantasy without interfering with the of laws free will. This would be close to virtual reality which will be the next major step in human evolution or technology to explain the fourth and fifth and eventually the seventh vibration.

As said in the foreword, everything starts in the mind and we can create the world we want to live in by the power of our minds. This is brought about by thought, desire, imagination and visualization simple but powerful.

So in the chamber of art and fantasy things are created to serve a purpose and when no longer desired they vanish. This is why it's important to play, as well as to work. As with all the killings going on in your world which at one time vibrations shifted to when this could be acted out in fantasy through TV films. This has happened but sadly it has not cut down on the crime rate and if anything has increased it. So we do not encourage anything like violence in this chamber but we do act out some wonderful fantasies in the likes of plays films. There is a great interest in animated films and fantasies. As already pointed out there are no limits in this chamber or in any of the chambers.

As the planet shifts into the seventh vibration, people will not be encouraged into making violent films or games. Hence the great interest in animated film on the planet earth at present and the many messages that are encoded in these fun loving magical characters. Of course this will all evolve much further in time. But at least for now if humans could reach a stage where they could act out their fantasies in a fun loving harmless way this is a step forward. I'm glad that today children are not encouraged to play out violent games in the playground as violence only depicts violence even if it is only played out. What happened to the magic in the world?. People have got so materialistic in the last century that they have forgotten the magic in them. In this chamber we encourage all kinds of arts, sorcery, crafts, spells, potions and lotions, to fuel the imagination of everyone as everyone comes here once in a while. On the earthly plane this is acted out in our dreams, nightmares, imagination, visualisation, and meditation. People come here and act out any event or circumstance they wish. This is very real indeed. If for instance I want to paint a picture I will paint that which I want with my thoughts and feelings in and if I want to be part of that world I just painted I can do so. The nearest we get to that dream world in reality, is through astral projection or astral travelling (see chamber Transcending & Transformation), but with the shift in vibration we can very shortly have these experience in virtual reality. Indeed at present we can see this through video games e.g. computer and x box, but again a bit like the atom bomb the human will go the destructive path at least until the whole of the planet makes the shift. Some will go with this shift and some will not, but rest assured the planet will make this shift and is making it as I write and as I have already said with some catastrophic consequences. This may sound like a fantasy world and that's exactly what it is. When souls pass on in your world and have not yet reached the seventh vibration or even the fifth, their mind will keep them there. So as you think, so you are. But thankfully these souls are helped to move into the seventh vibration- Heaven or their Heaven if you like. This is what the ascended Master Jesus was talking about when he made reference to his Apostles "the kingdom of God is at hand". He was not referring to Heaven as a place, but a state of awareness, an awareness "as you think so you are". As you will with intent and without fear of judgement, you will get and this takes place in the chamber of transcending and transformation. The children of the future will be encouraged to use their minds more, as children have a wonderful mind, that's why the Harry Potter books and films have been so successful on earth at present and not just for kids but to bring the child out in adults as well. However one must be careful with our fantasies as we do not live in a Harry Potter or Peter Pan world, so one must not use their imagination to escape their responsibilities of the real world. One must use their imagination to go deep within their real world or their inner world. Remember I said, it's all in the mind (see quantum physic).

However, one may ask the question is this world real or is it a dream. Perhaps to answer this question, we should look at dreams and the Psychology of Dreams without going into too much detail. Ever since biblical time dreams have played an important part in the evolution of man partly because people believed that dreams were an indication of what was going to happen. The dreams we are mostly associated with are those of Daniel and David the prophets and the dream of the three wise men at the birth of Christ. However dreams and the beliefs of dreams do not entirely belong to a biblical time. Benjamin Franklin was a great believer in the power of dreams, finding answers in moments of sleep and often did so. However this is not always the case with everyone. Dreams can be so mixed up and most of the time when we wake up nothing makes sense. However that is not to say that there is still no message in our dreams because in truth our spirit guides will often communicate to us through our dreams. So it's important that we get enough sleep and rest, "perchance to sleep perchance to dream" a well known phrase. A technique used on prisoners in the Second World War by the Nazi, not allowing them to sleep to break their spirits. We must be allowed to dream even a little day dreaming never harmed anyone. Dreams play an important part in our whole physiological make up. Let's look now at the psychology of dreams and dreaming and why it's so important to dream.

Man as having seven vibrations, has seven bodies: the physical, the enteric, the astral, the mental, and the spiritual and each body has its own type of dream. The physical body is known in Western psychology as the conscious, the enteric body as the unconscious, and the astral body as the collective unconscious the physical body creates its own dreams. If your stomach is upset, a particular type of dream is created. If you are unhealthy or feverish, the physical body creates its own type of dream. One thing is certain i.e. the dream is created out of certain emotions and feelings. Physical discomfort or physical disease, creates its own realm of dreams, so a physical dream can even be stimulated from the outside. If for instance, someone put a wet cloth around your legs, while your sleeping and begin to dream, you may dream you are crossing a river, or you are out at sea. If you go to sleep in a warm comfortable bed you may dream that you are on the beach and so on.

If you have suppressed physical desire or if you have financial difficulties for instance, then there is every possibility that you will dream of winning the lotto. These are the dreams that belong to the physical body i.e. the conscious. When you remember your dream as a dream, it is not a dream in the same sense as the dreams of the physical body. The enteric body can go out of you when you are asleep (see astral projection). Your physical body will be there, but your enteric body can go out and travel in space. Because the seven bodies are in existence simultaneously, something from one realm can pass into another and can penetrate it. This is known as the astral dream i.e. collective unconscious. In the first body, the physical, you can travel in neither time nor space. You are confined to your physical state and to the particular time it is say, ten o'clock at night. Your physical body can dream in this particular time and space, but not beyond it. In the enteric body you can travel in space but not in time. You can go anywhere, but the time is still ten o'clock at night. In the astral realm, in the third body, you can travel not only in space but also in time, into the past and the future. The astral body can pass the barrier of time. In psychology, the astral mind is called the collective unconscious. Through collective consciences, all myths of creation have been developed. They are all the same. The symbols differ, the stories differ a little bit, but whether they are Christian, Hindu, Jewish or Egyptian, the myths of creation i.e. how the world was created, how it came into existence, are all parallel; they all have many similarities. For example, similar stories of the great flood exist all over the world. There is no historical record of them but, still, there is a record. That record belongs to the spiritual body or collective consciences the seventh vibration. So when someone goes deep in meditation and sees colours, and experiences perfumes and sounds and music absolutely unknown, these are dreams, dreams of the enteric body i.e. unconscious of the seventh vibration and are quite real and indeed are real in the seventh vibration. But because we have only searched the mind at one level of existence, the physiological, and these dreams have either been interpreted in the language of the physiological or discarded, neglected. Or, put into the unconscious. However, to say that anything is part of the unconscious is really just to admit that we do not know anything about it. It is a technicality, a trick. Nothing is unconscious, but everything that is conscious on a deeper level is unconscious on the previous level, i.e. meditation. So for the physical, the enteric is unconscious; for the enteric, the astral is unconscious; for the astral, the mental is unconscious. Conscious means that which is known. Unconscious means that which is still not known, the unknown.

At this point I will leave you with some Energy Play Exercises to lighten things up after that last paragraph, so don't go out of your mind trying to understand all of this; simply remember that conscious means that which is known, unconscious means that which is still not known, the unknown.

Visualization,

When you visualise something, you use your five senses in your mind. If you want someone to call you, sit down and relax. Breathe and then visualise them on the phone ringing (sound) and see (sight) you going to the phone and picking it up. Feel (Touch) the coolness of the telephone. Smell (Smell) the pot of flowers near the telephone. That is basically visualisation.

To explain and take the visualization or fantasy a little further;

Visualize your spine as an antenna. The top is at the crown chakra; the bottom is at the base Chakra. Straighten your posture and shift your body until you find comfort and your connection with the earth. It may take only moments or you may have to work with it as you learn to attune yourself with Mother Earth. Take your time, when you are ready to proceed with the meditation take two or three deep, cleansing breaths. With each breath out, release any tension or anxiety in your body. Imagine yourself confined within a cocoon or as a small acorn. Your base Chakra is pressed against the bottom of the cocoon and you feel the warmth of the sun above you. Your base Chakra puts out a small root that descends from the bottom of this chakra. It makes its way between grains of rich, warm, damp earth, stopping every now and then to sample a delicious bit of pure, clean water. Soon the root comes upon an underground stream of remarkable purity and sweetness. As it sucks it up you feel the coldness of the water. It invigorates you and fills you with the earth's renewable energy. The top of your head sends a spurt of light from your crown chakra. It pushes its way up emerging into the warm sunlight. Deep in the earth, the root divides growing in all directions; providing a secure base for you each time. Nourishment is sucked into the physical body to invigorate it and strengthens it. Now the sun is warming on your head as sunlight is absorbed and turned into energy the top of the head is warm, almost hot, as the fire of the distant sun rains down. This makes the body feel taller as if it was growing upwards its roots branch out further. And with each breath you take, the body will feel much taller and lighter. Some visualise the body as a giant oak, and visualise their arms as branches but any visualization is fine. I myself prefer to use the image of a tree. Now at some point this body has reached its ultimate. Now there is more nourishment than the body needs. The crown Chakra opens and a fine blue mist rises from the top of the head. Beneath you, solid and protective, Mother Earth provides the base upon which your body exists. Feel the way your roots have sunk deep into the earth. Taste the elements that rise to nourish your body. Experience the feeling of being filled with energy. All your needs are met and there is energy left to spare. That which is not needed pours from your crown Chakra. From this you can fashion all things magical.

Continue to cycle energy through your body. Feel the effects of earth, water, air and fire. Then, when you are ready to return, begin to withdraw your roots, first a few, then some more. You find the energy that shot high into the sky from your crown Chakra is just that which you need. As the energy continues to diminish, you begin to shrink. Your branches pull back until your arms appear. Your roots contract until your feet stand upon the ground. You stand alone upon the field where once a mighty oak stood. But you have changed. You are no longer the tiny acorn You have experienced the power of earth, water, air, and fire. At any time you wish you could return to this place. You can reach deep into the earth for nourishment, take long drinks of pure water, feel the touch of the breeze and feel the strength of the sun. And from each you can weave a creative power and a connection to the Divine. Plan on spending 20 - 30 minutes the first time you do this meditation. The more often you do it, the faster it goes. I at one time did this once a day for a week. The following week I did it twice a day. The third week I did it three times a day. I was not spending more than a few minutes at a time on it by then. My next challenge was to do it as often as I could and eventually be able to do it on an in breath and an out breath. The goal is to learn to be grounded and centred at all times in all situations. If you work at this you can eventually achieve a state where you will no longer notice that you are grounded and centred. You will, instead, only notice when you are not grounded and centred, perhaps being drawn into some drama upsetting you. The more you practice staying calm the better you become at it.

The minds magical powers at work here are real. They aren't of some astral plane. They're within the Earth and they maintain life. We daily deplete our store of energy and replenish it through the air we breathe, the food we eat, and the powers that stream down from the Sun and Moon. Know that this power is physical. Yes, it's mysterious, but only because so few investigate it in magical ways.

Calm yourself, breathe deeply, and rub your palms together for 20 seconds. Start slowly and rub faster and faster. Feel your muscles tense. Feel your palms grow warm. Then suddenly, stop and hold your palms about 2 inches from each other. Feel them tingling... That's a manifestation of power! By rubbing your palms together and using the muscles in your arms and shoulders you're raising energy magical power. It's flowing from your palms as you hold them apart. Remember don't force yourself to feel the power. Trying harder won't accomplish anything. Relax and allow yourself to feel what's been there all the time. After you've actually sensed this energy, begin to fashion it into shapes. Use your visualization to do this. Directly after rubbing your hands, while they're still tingling, visualize jolts of energy perhaps electric blue or purple passing from your right (projective) palm to your left (receptive) palm. (If you are left handed, reverse the directions). Now envision this energy slowly swirling in a clockwise direction between your palms. Form it into a ball of glowing, pulsating magical energy. See its dimensions, its colours, textures, even smells. Feel its force and heat in your palms. There's nothing supernatural about it. Cup your hands around the ball. Make it grow or decrease in size through your visualization. Finally push it into your stomach and absorb it back into your system. Yes, you've done this with you mind, but also with power. Energy is real, and your ability to manipulate energy determines the effectiveness of your practice. Work with feeling and directing the power daily. Make this a sort of magical play until you reach the point you won't have to stop and think, "Can I do it? Can I raise the power? Can I help this planet?

You know, you can!

Greetings

Chapter 8

Chamber of Connection

This is the chamber where all the energy is studied. This is the link between the physical world and spirit world or the link between the fifth and seventh vibration. The is the place of atonement, meditation, visualization, magnetic fields, meridians lines auras, spirit guides (see chamber of healing & Guides) body energy centre etc- but better known as Charka. *Chakra is a Sanskrit word meaning wheel, or vortex, and it refers to each of the seven energy centres of which our consciousness, our energy system, is composed.*

These Chakras, or energy centres, function as pumps or valves, regulating the flow of energy through our energy system. The functioning of the Chakras reflects decisions we make concerning how we choose to respond to conditions in our life. We open and close these valves when we decide what to think and what to feel, and through these perceptual filters we choose to experience the world around us.

The Chakras are not physical. They are aspects of consciousness in the same way that the auras are aspects of consciousness. The Chakras are more dense than the auras, but not as dense as the physical body. They interact with the physical body through two major vehicles, the endocrine system and the central nervous system. Each of the seven Chakras is associated with one of the seven endocrine glands, and also with a group of nerves called a plexus. Thus, each Chakra can be associated with particular parts of the body and particular functions within the body. Thus, they are controlled by that plexus or that endocrine gland associated with that Chakra.

All of your senses, all of your perceptions, all of your possible states of awareness, everything it is possible for you to experience, can be divided into seven categories. Each category can be associated with a particular Chakra. Thus, the Chakras represent not only particular parts of your physical body, but also particular parts of your consciousness.

When you feel tension in your consciousness, you feel it in the Chakra associated with that part of your consciousness experiencing the stress, and in the parts of the physical body associated with that Chakra. Where you feel the stress depends upon why you feel the stress. The tension in the Chakra is detected by the nerves of the plexus associated with that Chakra, and transmitted to the parts of the body controlled by that plexus. When the tension continues over a period of time, or at a particular level of intensity, the person creates a symptom on the physical level.

The symptom speaks a language that reflects the idea that we each create our reality, and the metaphoric significance of the symptom becomes apparent when the symptom is described from that point of view. Thus, rather than saying, "I can't see," the person would describe it as keeping themselves from seeing something. "I can't walk," means the people have been keeping themselves from walking away from a situation in which they are unhappy. And so on.

The symptom served to communicate to the person through their body what they had been doing to themselves in their consciousness. When the person changes something about their way of being, getting the message communicated by the symptom, the symptom has no further reason for being, and it can be released, according to whatever the person allows themselves to believe is possible.

I believe everything is possible.

I believe that anything can be healed. It's just a question of how to do it.

Understanding the Chakras allows you to understand the relationship between your consciousness and your body, and to see your body as a map of your consciousness. It gives you a better understanding of yourself and those around you.

The Seventh Chakras

The following is a general summary of my current understanding of the physical locations and elements associated with each Chakra. Over the years I have noticed some minor discrepancies between how different people "define" each Chakra, (particularly the second and third Chakras) but the differences have only been minor. Certainly the colours and locations of the Chakras have always been consistent. The base Chakra extends down and the crown Chakra extends up...the Chakras in between have vortexes both to the front of the body and to the back.

The first Chakra is located at the base of the spine which is associated with smell, individuality, security, health and courage.

It is the Chakra that governs our physical existence, our bodies and our health. It is associated with the adrenal gland and controls the skeleton, nervous system, sense of smell, strong and flexible spine, bones, teeth, and nails it is associated with stability, stillness grounding and courage. This Chakra vibrates to the colour of red, the colour of passion and vitality.

The second Chakra is located in the area of the womb for woman or prostates or thereabouts for men, *associated* with taste, emotions, desire, pleasure and change.

It is associated with the gonad glands, sexual organs and control the sense of taste, the reproductive organs, kidneys and bladder feet and legs. It is also associated with enthusiasm, creativity, relationships, fear and anger. This Chakra vibrates to the colour of orange, the colour of creativity and desire.

The third Chakra is located at the solar plexus, assisting sight, energy, radiance, power and self-control.

It is associated with the pancreas and controls the sense of sight, the autonomic nervous system, lower back, muscles, liver, spleen, stomach, gall bladder and the digestive system. It is also associated with self- control, vitality and inner strength. . This Chakra vibrates to the colour of yellow, the colour of power and inner strength.

The fourth Chakra (the middle chakra in the chain of seven) is the heart chakra, associated with touch, unconditional love, forgiveness, compassion, and balance.

It is associated with the colour green, and also the colour rose, which is the "colour of love." This Chakra is connected with emotion and human love. It is associated with the thymus gland and controls the sense of touch, the heart, breasts, vaguest nerve, the blood circulation and the immune and endocrine system. It is also associated with peace, harmony, unconditional love and personal transformation. This Chakra vibrates to the colour of green, the colour of growth and transformation

The fifth Chakra is located at the throat and is a bright blue, aids hearing, communication, kindness, truth and loyalty.

It governs communication and personal magnetism. It is the chakra that most influences intercommunication and our "personas." It is also the link between emotion and thought. It is associated with thyroid gland and controls the lymphatic system the metabolism, hands, arms, shoulders, mouth, vocal cords, lungs, bronchial system, sense of sound the throat neck and voice. It is associated with self-expression confidence and truth. This Chakra vibrates to the colour of blue, the colour of communication and healing.

The sixth Chakra is located at the third eye (mid-forehead) and is indigo deep purple blue, which is responsible for Intuition Clairvoyance, Imagination and Perception.

This Chakra is associated with thought (though some say the third chakra governs thought) and with vision, particularly psychic vision. It is also the chakra of spiritual love and connection. It is responsible for Intuition Clairvoyance, Imagination and Perception). This will open up your psychic and your third eye chakra, and there will be a great sense of peace flowing through you, which may come as messages from your guide or guides etc. It is associated with the pituitary gland and controls the left eye, lower brain, nose, ears and the endocrine system. This Chakra vibrates to the colour of indigo or light purple the colour of unity and wisdom.

The seventh Chakra is at the crown of the head, and is violet fading to white further away from the body associated infinite, oneness with the infinite and Divine wisdom.

This Chakra is our connection to our "higher selves" and to the "Divine." It is associated with wisdom and integration of our eternal selves with our current physical selves. It is like our umbilical cord to "God."
It is associated with the pineal gland and controls the right eye upper brain and central nervous system and unity with the divine and universal consciousness. This Chakra vibrates to the colour of white, the colour of purity and light.

When all the Chakras are "whirling," open, bright and clean, then our Chakra system is balanced. When a Chakra becomes blocked, damaged, or muddied with residual energy, then our physical and emotional health can be affected. Often this occurs habitually as the result of negative or incomplete belief systems. The effects of our habits, feelings, beliefs, thoughts, fears and desires can be found in our Chakras.

For example, if you eat poorly (a lot of processed food, for instance) and don't exercise, chances are your root (red) Chakra is going to become sluggish, darkened and dull. If you "close off" your emotions because they're painful or overwhelming, your heart Chakra is likely to become tight and closed and block emotional energy. If you, on the other hand, are extremely centred in your intellect, you may have a bulging and bright third eye Chakra but a disproportionately small heart Chakra or root Chakra or womb Chakra. Or perhaps you're cerebrally focused on finding answers to deep questions about reality. In the West we tend to value the upper Chakras over the lower Chakras. This probably has it's roots in our ancestors' religious aversion to the "flesh" and their focus on the rewards of "heaven."

The goal is a strong, clear, balanced energy system. The more open and clearly balanced the Chakras are the more energy can flow through your system. This energy is essential for vitality, health, and continued spiritual growth. As people connect again to their true essence, which is happening at present on your earth through the many forms of alternative live style, this shift can be speeded up ten fold. And this is what is really happening at present. People are studying various types of meditation etc which will stop them searching outside of themselves and they will look inward for the true essence. Even technology is playing its part here, as the Internet in the major way of connecting people together. So it is no longer a connection of little towns, villages and neighborhoods, it is now a connection of towns cities and countries and indeed the whole planet. This is the first step to real spiritual connection where all souls are equal and special so we have evolved to bring this about. But what really helps with all of this is the understanding of the body's energy system, the outer esoteric bodies i.e. Chakras and Aura that connect people to their true essence. This knowledge will link us to the seventh vibration, which will bring about true spiritual connection. These Chakras or vortex as they are known in the Chamber Connection, play a major part in the connections of spirit and physical and a major part in the different vibrations, to help us to develop the many gifts we have. Let me explain.

We know that all down through human evolution that people practiced physic phenomena i.e. the occult, and to most people this would be regarded as supernatural or even evil practice. Here we need to set things straight. As with all gifts and abilities, it depends on how we use them as we all have them and we all have free will of course. In the seventh vibration we learn to use our free will wisely and for the good of all. To give you an example of these physic abilities here are just a few clairvoyance, clairaudience etc.

All of these gifts, that some might call supernatural abilities, and what we are seeing at present on our planet through the many lightworkers and will continue to see in the future will be regarded as natural abilities in time to come. Indeed most of us are aware of the five senses taste, sight, speech, hearing and touch. We accept these gifts as normal, however, take an example of someone born without the gift of sight they would never be able to describe a rose in its full beauty. They would be able to feel its textures and smell its lovely scent, but they would never be able to truly describe its beauty. They would not be able to see the wonderful colour of the flower, which most of us take for granted and accept as natural. So, anyone who has developed the psychic power of clairvoyance and the like which is indeed a wonderful talent but to those who have developed these gifts, it is just natural.

As we advance forward with the help of science and psychic talents, we will understand these gifts much more clearly and will realise that we always had them just like dogs and cats, which are very psychic. We have however over the last few hundred years or so lost these wonderful abilities mainly due to the fact that we became more materialistic and mechanical. We eventually did not need these talents, as we no longer had to hunt for our survival. So we eventually moved further away from nature and natures rituals. However, some who were still curious or perhaps indeed afraid of the rest of us who were still practicing these gifts outside in woodland areas, were not happy. They tried to put an end to these practices by slaughtering the majority to bring us under control. When everything was under control after many years of crusading they built big buildings with very little light coming in i.e. Churches and Temples etc. So we were eventually moved away from outside worship with the result that, the angelical energy of the sunrays i.e. the rays of the seventh vibration or, the energy of the angelica kingdom- could not penetrate our world. It was a very dark time indeed. We weren't even allowed to celebrate Christmas.

Oh yes Christmas goes back a lot further that the Christ child. The history of Christmas dates back over 4000 years. Many of our Christmas traditions were celebrated centuries before the Christ child was born. The 12 days of Christmas, the bright fires, the Yule log, the giving of gifts, carnivals (parades) with floats, carollers who sing while going from house to house, the holiday feasts, and the church processions can all be traced back to the early Mesopotamians. . The exact day of the Christ child's birth has never been pinpointed. Traditions say that it has been celebrated since the year 98 AD. In 137 AD the Bishop of Rome ordered the birthday of the Christ Child celebrated as a solemn feast. In 350 AD another Bishop of Rome, Julius I, choose December 25th as the observance of Christmas.

Many of these traditions began with the celebration of the festival of New Year .The Mesopotamians believed in many gods. The Persians and the Babylonians celebrated a similar festival called the Sacaea. The early Europeans believed in evil spirits, witches, ghosts and trolls. As the Winter Solstice approached, with its long cold nights and short days, many people feared the sun would not return. Special rituals and celebrations were held to welcome back the sun. In Scandinavia during the winter months the sun would disappear for many days. After thirty-five days scouts would be sent to the mountaintops to look for the return of the sun. When the first light was seen the scouts would return with the good news. A great festival would be held, called the Yuletide, and a special feast would be served around a fire burning with the Yule log. Great bonfires would also be lit to celebrate the return of the sun. In some areas people would tie apples to branches of trees to remind themselves that spring and summer would return.

The ancient Greeks held a festival similar to that of the Persian festivals Sacaea to assist their god Kronos who would battle the god Zeus and his Titans. The Roman's celebrated their god Saturn. Their festival was called Saturnalia which began the middle of December and ended January 1st. With cries of "Jo Saturnalia!" the celebration would include masquerades in the streets, big festive meals, visiting friends, and the exchange of good-luck gifts called Strenae (lucky fruits). The Romans decked their halls with garlands of laurel and green trees lit with candles. Again the masters and slaves would exchange places. "Jo Saturnalia!" was a fun and festive time for the Romans, but the Christians thought it an abomination to honour the pagan god. The early Christians wanted to keep the birthday of their Christ child a solemn and religious holiday, not one of cheer and merriment as was the pagan Saturnalia. But as Christianity spread they were alarmed by the continuing celebration of pagan customs and Saturnalia among their converts. At first the Church forbid this kind of celebration. But it was to no avail. Eventually it was decided that the celebration would be tamed and made into a celebration fit for the Christian Son of God. Some legends claim that the Christian "Christmas" celebration was invented to compete against the pagan celebrations of December. The 25th was not only sacred to the Romans but also the Persians whose religion Mithraism was one of Christianity's main rivals at that time. The Church eventually was successful in taking the merriment, lights, and gifts from the Saturanilia festival and bringing them to the celebration of Christmas

This shift to move the people to worshipping inside in semi dark buildings for whatever feast they celebrate such as the festival of Christmas, is only given as an example of human evolution and it had an enormous effect on our psyche. The Angelica energy now could not get through and this closed down the working of the Chakras and reduced the size of the pineal gland associated with our third eye, which is known as our psychic gland. However, they did not stop there. They almost closed down many wonderful pagan rituals i.e. Easter and Christmas but as mentioned in the above paragraph the old school of thought won the day. However, they even went as far as to eventually close down the pineal gland by making religious rituals on our forehead. This is still practiced today partly to keep us in control but mostly practiced out of fear. This certainly had its meaning 4000 years ago, but as we know a little knowledge is dangerous. At that time, we would not have been able to handle this inner sight and those that had it, mostly took a negative road and others did not stay long on this planet i.e. saints. So everything has a purpose, this is how we evolved. Those that held on to these abilities went underground until such a time as evolution would come about again, when these gifts of connecting people to spirit would be encouraged once again. The time has now come when we can go back to the old school of thought, but this time not out of fear ignorance or superstition or out of fear or ego within the church and many religions sects, but out of knowledge and wisdom of Divine light.

At this time now in our evolution we are encouraged once again to practice meditation and to get out into nature and absorb the suns rays, which is the Angelica ray or the golden rays (see sun gazing). This is the eighth rays; which hasn't yet reached our planet, well not in full splendour. However, the planet in the last decade or so has been bombarded every so often with this golden ray and Angels are everywhere. There are healers all over the planet at present, who work closely with the Angelic kingdom. This is the energy that will connect every soul together as one and although technology is indeed playing it's part, it is almost the time when we have to make another shift away from technology, especially the push button scene. It is almost the time that we move away completely from machinery as mankind has only used this information, mostly to kill .We have to move or shift our awareness into a new source of energy, as I mentioned earlier, as a lot of our resources are used up now on the planet. Most of it was wasted fighting wars and killing our inner spirit. As I said in the last chapter; in the seventh vibration all souls are one.

The new energy we will be heading towards is simple light i.e. Crystal light. Even this computer which I write this book on is controlled by light i.e. electronics, and fragments of Crystals which in the future will enhance electricity. Oh yes electricity has always been around but since the invention of the electric light in the 1920's Thomas Edison a motion picture camera and phonograph, who was in the field of psychic research, busily at work in his laboratory building a machine to achieve Spirit communication when he invented the electric light.

In the future with the shift in collective coconsciousness we will go beyond electricity itself, simply working on pure light. When you think of it from the manufacture of the first computer we have definitely moved on as most computers now are voice activated but we will go beyond this. In fact in the seven vibrations everyone will communicate by telepathy so our minds will resort back to be once again the greatest computers. This is the real power to connect and this gifts and it will be developed quite quickly by the introduction of the 12 strand DNA strands that are being transmuted to all souls since the year 2000. This however will not be quite recognized by our scientists till the year 2012 and indeed some will not discover their psychic abilities until much later. This is all brought about by the shift in awareness and the golden energy from the Angelica realms. In the seventh vibration, everyone will have the gift of telepathy and everyone will have ability to communicate telepathically with each other on many dimensions. As governments, heads of churches and cares of states develop these gifts, we will never be able to lie to one another again. So the element of fear will be banished from our planet forever and everyone will have the power to connect. So conversation with someone from another realm (spirit world) will be as easy as a telephone call is to us, now in the third vibration. It's important now more than ever, that we humans have a little knowledge of meditation and visualization skills, as it is these skills that will set us on the next stage of our evolutionary journey. We are no longer separated as there is no separation from me to you or from them to us. There is no separation. It is only an illusion brought about by our pride and by our egotistic minds. So with the invention of electricity which was indeed a most profound invention by a man of vision and probably one of the greatest inventors of the 21st century? Indeed this invention has come about at the right time as nothing happens by chance, to prepare us for the next quantum leap into the seventh vibration.

Here now are some exercises that you can try to get connected.

Meditation Exercises to connect

1. Sit in a straight-backed chair, supporting your lower back with a pillow if necessary. Your chin should be tucked in slightly level with the floor, eyes closed, back straight, hands resting on your knees, palms up and fingers relaxed. In this position you should be comfortable and relaxed, the spine straight and the torso erect.

2. Breathe deeply for several minutes. Relax. Forget. Visualize the multitude of tensions and worries of your everyday life exiting your body with your breath. Relax into the chair.

3. Now open your consciousness. Allow your conscious mind to be receptive and alert. Commune and talk with inner mind or guides. Toss around symbols in your head. If you wish, chant one of the names of your favorite Saint or guide or your own name. This is an excellent tool for getting beyond the third vibration'

Note:
Select your time and place for meditation with care. Light should be subdued; candlelight is excellent. Burn white or blue candles if you wish. A bit of incense is fine too, but too much smoke can (obviously) cause problems during deep breathing. Immediately after each meditation session, record all images, thoughts and sensations in a notebook.

Visualization Exercises

Exercise One:
Sit or lie comfortably with your eyes shut. Relax you body. Breathe deeply and still your mind. Pictures will continue to pop into your head. Choose one of these and stick with it. Let no images intrude other than the one you've chosen. Keep all thoughts revolving around the image. Retain this picture for as long as you can, then let it go and end the exercise. When you can retain one picture for more than a few minutes, move onto the next step.

Exercise Two:
Decide upon an image to hold and retain it within your mind. You might wish to have it physically present and study it first, memorizing each detail-the way shadows play on it, its textures, colours, perhaps even a scent. You might choose a small three-dimensional shape, such as a pyramid, or something more complex such as an image of a purple candle or a ripe apple. After studying it thoroughly, close your eyes and see the object before them-just as if your eyes were open. Don't look at the object again with your physical eyes but with your magical imagination-with your powers of visualization. When you can hold this image perfectly for five minutes, move on.

Exercise Three:
This is more difficult, and is truly magical in nature. Visualize something, anything, but preferably something you've never seen before. For instance, let's use a candle. It's purple, ten feet tall covered with yellow lines around it. This is just an example of course. Now close your eyes and see this ten-foot candle in your mind. It's never existed. You're creating it with your visualization, your magical imagination. Make the candle real. Turn it over in your mind so that you can see it from all angles. Then let it vanish. When you can hold any such self-created image for about five minutes or so, continue on to the next exercise.

Exercise Four:

This is the most difficult. Hold a self-created image (such as the ten foot purple candle) in your mind with your eyes open. Work at keeping it visible and real, Stare at a wall, look at the sky, or gaze at a busy street, but see the candle there. Make it so real you can touch it. Try having it rest on a table or sitting on the flour.

Note:
If we're to use visualization to create changes in this world, not in the shadowy realm that exists behind our eyelids, we must practice such techniques with our eyes open. The true test of visualization lies in our ability to make the visualized object (or structure) real and a part of our world. When you've perfected this exercise, you're well on your way!

In the chamber of connection, which governs all the abilities and ways, we here on earth have in order to connect to our inner world, remember the kingdom of God is within. Communication has never completely broken but perhaps it's a bit like a bad connection on your radio. The connection was still there but, we just couldn't get the correct station. As we emerge into more light i.e. lightworkers we will be able to make this connection to almost any realm we choose, and to people who have passed from this world. We will be easily able to contact them just by thought i.e. telepathy. Indeed telepathy is going to be the next major step in our evolutionary journey as we emerge into the light. The chamber of connection will send rays of light every 3 to 6 months to our planet so there will soon be a major shift in human evolution. This shift will probably not emerge fully on our planet till the year 2097 but this all depends on our willingness to open up our awareness to these possibilities that all things are possible on the seventh vibration. As we emerge more into the light that is already working on our planet, we will understand the old mystery of death and what happens after and where do souls go. I said in my last book "A way to Healing", that death was like taking a journey but the physical body doesn't go with us. It is perhaps like a journey into another country. Take for example if you went to another country to live and your parents went a few months years before you. I'm sure that before you left to go on your journey you would ring them and tell them, you were coming to see them or perhaps you would leave some word with a friend regarding when you would arrive there. On your arrival, do you not think that they would be there to meet you? It is most likely they would, especially if they knew you were coming.

Then after some time in your new place and new surrounding, a few months or years you would eventually forget all about the country you left. Indeed you wouldn't worry about those you left at home, Earth, because you would be fully aware that they have their own path and anyway they would be over to see you shortly as in this realm there is no such thing as time. Indeed as we advance into the light with the many gifts and insights we will develop, speeded up of course by the practice of meditation and sun gazing (see chamber of crystal) and alternative life style etc. We will have a better understanding of how human evolution came about and for what purpose. We will realize that we have, and always had, the power to transcend and to connect to a kinder spirit, the spirit within. We will realise that life here on earth, is indeed really an illusion, but in the seventh vibration it is very real. Everything is created by our mind i.e. our thoughts and everything is connected to all other minds or the infinite mind.

Perhaps at this point, all of this may be getting much more in-depth, or and esoteric than is fitting for a human mind to grasp at this stage of evolution. So I'll leave any further speculations, and ponderings to you, for another time. This chapter and indeed this whole book is intended mostly to give you something to think about, to open your mind to an awareness of collective consciousness. It is then up to you to keep, or discard, as you feel impressed to do so. Remember nothing is impossible in the seventh vibration.

Do not separate yourselves from me to you, or from them to us as we are all connected; stay connected.

Greetings.

Chapter 9

Chamber of Transcending & Transformation

By reading over the last chapter one might say that we're heading into exciting times indeed, but we are not heading into anything. We are living in exciting times. This is indeed the time of transcending and transformation and a lot of preparation has been done for this time on our planet. This work is carried out mostly by other worlds that have representatives in the chamber of council. In this chamber representatives of other worlds like Pleiades, Sirius and of course Arcturus have a strong interest in earths evolution, so they have created a new vortex of energy for the planet earth to evolve. Perhaps it would be advisable at this stage to explain to the reader what is meant by a vortex so you have a better understanding of how change has come about and how change is unavoidable.

So what is a vortex, anyway? Well you see them in everyday life. The turbulent flow of water makes vortices. If you have ever seen a whirlpool in a river or watched water going down the drain in the bathtub, you have seen a vortex. A vortex is created from spiralling motion of air, liquid or gas around a centre of rotation. If you have ever witnessed a dust storm kick up in the desert, either in real life or on the TV you have seen a vortex. In many places throughout the planet, vortexes are created, not by wind or water, but from spiralling spiritual energy. Vortex sites are believed to be spiritual locations where the energy is right to facilitate prayer, meditation and healing and believed to be locations having energy flow that exists on multiple dimensions. The energy of the vortexes interacts with a person's inner self. It is not easily explained. Obviously it must be experienced.

So a vortex is a funnel like structure it has many functions but it usually works like a waste disposal machine. There are many types of vortex or portholes as they are sometimes called; one connecting the earth crystal core and two connecting the inner Angelica realms. At this present time in the earth's evolutionary history those vortex e.g. that were encoded by the higher super beings of the Angelica world are more active and spinning a lot faster that ever before. These vortexes of funnel allowed the residue of negative energy to be transformed to positive energy, to be filtered down, to be purified only to rise again. In doing so this raises the vibration and awareness on a collective conscious level on our planet and indeed raise's the vibrations of the whole galaxy. This is the shift that everyone talks about i.e. 2012 but remember what ever happens in this time depends on the collective mind of everyone, as one mind affects another and eventually affecting all minds. So its important to stay positive in our thoughts in this period of tribulations known as the seven year tribulation.

The shift is very recognisable at present and indeed almost tangible as many changes and transformations come about.

At present on our planet we have moved away from the Piscean age, which is to do with the fish, to the Aquarian age, which is to do with a new code of energy. This energy is being filtered down directly from the higher realms of inner light i.e .the source from the Chamber of Transcending and Transformation, to transform humanity on the lower plains. Indeed as mentioned in my introduction this new ray of energy is the purple ray of purification of the masculine and feminine energies intertwining the blue of the masculine energy and the pink of the feminine energy as the feminine energy at present is ascending on the planet. We are now moving out of the male masculine dominant energies to the more subtle female energies as our planet mother earth is ascending. As the vibrations of the planet shift we also shift in the vibrations and a vortex is open. This vortex is one that allows the collective consciousness that holds negative energy to be separated from the consciousness that holds positive energy. In other words it's the vortex that is put in place to transform fear and ignorance to compassion and love, because without love nothing can evolve. This vortex, that is now open, has made many of the lightworkers more aware of the plains that exist beyond the seventh vibration and beyond the higher Ascended Master, connecting them to the plains of other Crystalline beings, super beings or, i.e. lords of light, the council of high priest and the cosmic Devas. These higher beings are now coming into the inner space of the planet making their energy of transformation, light and wisdom available to each and everyone of us as we move out of the 3 – D time frame, into a more multi-dimensional time frame.

Since the beginning of this millennium many lightworkers have made the ascent and are helping others to follow closely behind. As mentioned previously the masculine energies and the feminine energies are interwoven in a vortex of the purple flame of purification encoded by St Germain and Merlin the magician of the inner realms. Since 2007 it is more active on our planet. This was a major step to bring this invocation of light into the physical world and restore the plan for earth that was originally constructed by the lords of light from the chamber of council that oversee everything concerning this galaxy. This is an extremely important time in the process of human evolution and the evolution of other worlds as many are waiting and watching with caution. We are in a way being used as an example for the lower realms to speed up evolution. So humans are going through the greatest changes in evolutionary history and they will have to be able to connect to the higher Celestials Realms of love and light, to the newly accessible realms of the fairy world and nature realms.

I said earlier that many of the lightworkers have made the shift from a 3-D reality of the third vibrations to a more accessible quantum perspective of the seventh vibration time frame. The higher energies of the Celestials inner Realms of the solar star system are more subtle than they have been in the past.

The subtle energies that are being transmitted to the earth from the higher dimensions are changing. The alignments in the heavens are different and the energies transmitted from the star systems are of a higher, more powerful frequency. These energies change the way matter relates to spirit and the way the physical world relates to the spiritual. These waves of light are having the effect of raising our vibration, assisting us in connecting with the higher aspects of our being, expanding our consciousness and accelerating our spiritual growth. We see from our last chapter that we can connect with these energies easily through meditation, awakening our light bodies, by blending with our soul and by opening our channel upwards to the higher dimensions. We are going to look at how these exciting energies are going to affect our lives and how we can use them to best assist us in the next part of our evolutionary journey. These subtle energies that are at present being filtered down to earth are in a way very powerful and many lightworkers are fully aware of these energies and the changes they'll bring about.

Their effects have been building up prior to the start of this century and will be felt over the next one hundred years or so. This light will affect us all in different ways. The light I'm talking about of course is not physical light but what many scientists call frozen light (see quantum physics). Over the course of time people's lives will change and the way we relate to the spiritual world will be different. At one level we may feel the effects as an increased desire to slow down, to take time off, spend more time outside enjoying and appreciating nature, being reflective and enjoying those pursuits that make us take time out for ourselves. We may feel drawn to spend more time pursuing those things, which improve our health and vitality, such as meditation, yoga, tai- chi and other healing arts. We may want to add more beauty and harmony to our environment and bring increased order to all aspects of our lives. This is perhaps the first keynote of these energies, is that we are drawn to spend time on ourselves, to improve the quality of our inner and outer worlds and to do things that enhance our own self worth. The other noticeable change in vibrations is perhaps the number of people who are experiencing ailments at this time that doctors cannot identify with. This is not really because people are falling into bad health but it is because the physical world is changing frequency and we are not used to doing this in a conscious state. Many of the symptoms are like forgetfulness, headaches, much the same as migraine, lots of unusual aches and pains in the body that cannot be explained, problems with eyes, ears, nose and teeth. Also people feeling very tired, sensitive to a lot of noise, finding it hard to concentrate and in general out of sorts with the world around them. This is why it's important at this time that people would take up some form of relaxation therapy tai chi, yoga any meditation that will help to shift awareness and make the transition as easy as possible for as many people as possible, I stress this point. During this time of transition it's important that we get enough sleep and rest, vitamins, fruit and vegetables and an increased intake of water to cleanse the blood to act as a purifier for the kidneys. The kidneys are the shock absorbers of the body and blockage there will result in holding toxins in the body that may cause severer headaches or other illness.

However, those of you who have made the shift are already noticing changes. Some of you have discovered that indeed material things do not matter. You may do with less sleep, less food, and you will not be dictated to by the elements what to wear as you will be at one with the elements. Indeed some of you are emerging into new bodies, which are called the Crystalline bodies of the seventh vibration. I have already mentioned about these Crystallite body in my introduction (see introduction).

Many of you are noticing that you have become lighter and the lighter you become the more difficult it is too, to process the density of your past fears. This shift in awareness into the seventh vibration allows you to draw up all those dense aspects of yourself and allows you to stand in your own crystal body or your own power. You will realise now that life, your life and the other lives you lived, is a connection of many souls of a game being played on this stage we call earth in the drama of life itself. You will look at yourself now with new awareness, breaking away from the old consciousness that you have felt trapped in for so long over many life times. This is the power to connect. This of course seems to you to be only happening to a few but of course it's happening on a collective consciousness level and governments, churches and states and the world at large. Many will find themselves uniting and working together to ensure that the principle laws of the universe of right action are carried out. The governments of South Africa will go through some of its greatest changes for a long time. I give you an example of what happened in Zimbabwe. This will not happen like many transformations of the past which was done in darkness as, this will be done in light. If men of governments, church and state of the third vibration do not willingly welcome this shift and surrender to the light, they will fall and lose all power and indeed around the world there will be many changes in government.

I mentioned in the introduction that the royal family will go through some terrific changes that will surely rock their world and will help people to understand that no one thing, government, church or state can be ruled by one belief system. But it is the universal love and light that rules and resides in the heart of humans. This, not alone will affect governments, but it will affect churches as well and so many religious sectors through the world where practice and belief are based on fear and not out of love and compassion.

Those that are able to hold the light in this time of transformation will grow and continue to do so and those that are not will no longer have power. Ireland is one of the countries that will hold great consciousness and will be an example for many to follow and a great union of these energies with like-minded people who have chosen Ireland as a focal point and a place to work. This will take place in this country in the year 2012. From there on, these energies that are directed from the Ascended Masters will also lead us to greater spiritual awakening, encouraging people onto their spiritual path and moving those already on the path to far greater growth and awareness. We are finding it easier to connect with the higher parts of our being - our higher self, our soul, and the spirit within us. We are awakening our light bodies so that we can play effectively with the subtle energies and expand our consciousness. These energies stimulate us, increasing our psychic abilities, deepening our intuitive senses, opening our channel upwards and connecting us with the beings of light that are here to assist us. We are then able to channel their wisdom and guidance..

Another keynote of these waves of light and energy is that they add light to all aspects of our lives. They strengthen all those forms, structures and relationships that are working well and can hold light. This light makes those forms more cohesive, able to endure, grow and expand through these times.

As I said each aspect of our lives is made up of subtle energies and requires a certain setup of energies to remain stable and function well for us. As we feel the effects of the waves of energy transmitted to the planet raising our vibration, we may feel that the old energy set-ups are no longer in alignment with who we are. Another keynote of working with these energies is being willing to truly let go of those things that no longer serve us. By letting go of them easily it will seem like a gradual process of change. By trying to hold onto them when their time with us has passed can cause much turbulence and difficulty. We can know that nothing will leave our lives unless something much better is going to join us. Now is a very positive time to release the old forms and create new in our lives - these energies are very much supporting us in doing this.

We ourselves can focus this light on all our projects to add to their success. This focus will intensify these energies and can vastly increase our ability to manifest and create transformation. The forms that we create will be beyond our dreams in their expansiveness and power. These energies will also speed up the process of turning energy into matter and becoming form.

To create these results it is important for us to be willing to follow our inner urges - for this to is another keynote of these energies. . If we remain in tune with these energies, life can seem so easy and we can feel energised and supported at all times. If we ignore these inner messages life can seem a struggle. We often feel drained and our enthusiasm and sense of purpose will diminish.

An easy way to increase your sense of these subtle energies and indeed another keynote of this time is to increase your connection with your soul. Your soul is a part of your being that is with you at all times. Since the Enlightenment era and the writings of Descartes and other enlightenment philosophers, we have been led to focus on our sense of self as separate from others and separate from our soul. These energies are changing this belief and we are gradually shifting into a realisation that by connecting with our soul and carrying out its wishes and desires, life becomes a lot easier.

Our soul is a wise being of vast intelligence that wants what is best for us. It is concerned with our happiness, our growth and our evolution into the light. It is with us to assist with every aspect of our life and is always leading us to greater wholeness and love. It is an all-loving being of immense power. By consciously connecting with our soul through the day it is much easier to follow the energies. All you have to do is intend to make this blending with your soul, sense its love and light surrounding you and trust that the connection has been made.

Our soul can communicate with us by taking energy out of those things that no longer serve us and energising those paths that are for our highest good. It communicates through the still, quiet voice of our intuition, through our dreams, and by dropping thoughts into our mind giving us that sense of "aha". Our soul makes us feel positive and happy about those things that are right for us. If you are having difficulty deciding on which option to take in a certain situation, get quiet and tune into your soul. As you think of the choices available, get a sense of which choices you feel positive about, which feel light, joyful and expansive and seem to hold a lot of light. This is how your soul communicates what is best for you. The more often you do this process, the easier you will find this and it will always lead you to your highest good and greatest joy.

By increasing your connection with your soul you will notice that you feel and act in more loving ways - another keynote of these times. You will focus on what is good and beautiful about people and situations and your heart will go out to those in need. Instead of entering power struggles with people you will view them from a place of love and compassion, which allows you to act and think in different ways. This leads to an improvement in all your relationships at every level. During this turbulent time in the world we are constantly challenged to focus on people's good and see their beauty at a soul level.

From this state of compassion we are led on to another keynote - that of group consciousness and group works. People are getting together to hold a focus of love and light for the planet and all of humanity. They are networking and finding ways to work together for a greater good. The Internet is facilitating this change in our thinking. So much information is available on it for all and it is so easy for people from all over the world to share information, ideas and to unite. As we open our hearts we are able to see ourselves not as separate beings in a separatist world but as one, united in a shared consciousness. This will increase over the next one hundred years until humanity has shifted into a "heart centred" i.e. the seven vibration focusing these energies upon your goals and intentions, it is then important to follow your intuitive guidance and be open to the signs that are there to lead you in the right direction. You can use these energies to assist you with small things in your life as well as big projects. At all times there are energies that guide us to do certain things; all we have to do is ask.

Energy Projection

Well we're near the end of this book which I hope you enjoyed and which I hope you will share with others as we all make the next quantum leap onto the next part of our evolutionary journey. However, before I finish, I said I would leave some information on Astral projection which will be if you like your passport to linking up to the spirit realm time frame of the seven vibrations. Anyway, before we get into all of that, let's go back here a little and look at energy projection, which is much easier to understand if you consider that the body has three basic functions that at all times seek to be together. There are concentrations, or the point of the body on which the mind is centred, the weight, or the point of the body that is the centre of gravity and the energy focal point, the part of the body that is doing work at any particular time. The action of these three things trying to be together at all times allows us to control the point in the body or out from the body that the mind is centred on at all times.

The main way of projecting energy from the body is from the eyes. Energy can be projected from any point of the body but the eyes are naturally the largest energy projection point in the body. So it is by controlling the eyes that we learn to project energy from the body and as the eyes are the mirrors of the soul or the mind of a person we learn to recognise the energy changes in other people as well. This is a natural skill for most people as people will take one look at someone and say; "what's up with you"? But with the correct training one is able to take this recognition a little further and a good skilled lightworker/ healer or Doctor remember Doctors are healers as well, who have worked a long time on their own energy system through meditation / Qi gong etc is able to look into a person or persons eyes and know what is wrong with them physically, emotionally, mentally and spiritually. Indeed they are able to look into a person's eyes and know what is happening in that person's life. Many lightworkers, who have reached the seventh vibration, have this skill in abundance. To give an example here how energy is projected from the eyes, most of us will have at some stage, an experience of eyes meeting across a crowed room, emotional state of mind and intention being pre conveyed from the eyes Many souls have found life long relationships in these forms of manifestations, projecting strong emotional feelings through the eyes. There are different manifestations of energy and these energy manifestations are an outward expression of the energy patterns of the mind. If for instance you have what's known as the evil eye (which is not simply, someone throwing a bad look at you it is a lot more serious than that), it is sadly someone of a lower vibration working with spirit from the lower astral world (see astral) of evil intent. In the past pyschic powers were used for good as well as bad intent. It was said that a person with the evil eye could kill animals and even make people very sick from a distance just with their intent, not a practice to be encouraged so we'll say no more on that. Another example many people have is the experience of someone behind them looking at them and being able to feel their presence. What is really happening to them is that they are feeling the energy projection from the person eyes that is behind them, the stronger the emotion the greater the amount of energy that is projected. So the eyes indeed are projections of a person's energy or mind state and by controlling the state of the eyes we learn to control the state of the mind. In other words your energy state. So you can go from being very passive and uninvolved to explosively powerful and back to being passive again by triggering the bodies energy system a skill often practiced in advanced level of martial arts i.e. (Taiji). Although the use of the eyes is not eventually how it is done, it's how we can begin to understand the projection of energy by the eyes. After having learned how to project one's energy by using the eyes we can then project energy from any part of the body and eventually project our energy away from the body. This is known as Astral Projection. So the next part of our discussion takes us beyond energy projection to Astral projection, which basically deals with 'how to get out of your body' and deals with all the things you can do and meet on the Astral Plane, which has lower and higher vibration depending on your mind state?

Astral Projection is the projection of your mental body to any place outside your physical body. To do this, the mental body needs a part of your astral body to serve as its vehicle. It's not an unnatural thing to happen. In fact, we unconsciously do it two to four times at night, when we are asleep. Many little children for example report 'flying' dreams. Those weren't dreams, but astral projections. The real fun starts if we can train our being to astral project 'at will', or, in other words, when we are conscious. When you are consciously 'out there' (on the Astral Plane), you can go anywhere you want, see what you want to see, heal the sick, work some good and meet the other beings on the Astral Plane; the elementals, the guides, other Astral travellers, earthbound spirits and Angels etc in fact carry out any fantasy you wish.

Astral Projection, how to do it?.

There are many ways to achieve Astral Projection. In fact, there are about as many different ways as there are practitioners. Shamans may call up the help of nature spirits to take him out of his body. Some healers call on their Angels to assist them in their spirit vision' rituals. So, there's not one way to do it. Please remember this as you go along and feel free to make any adjustments you want to make to the following meditation. As long as it 'feels right', you're doing fine. The meditation in this text, however, was designed to more or less 'bridge' the different methods used in astral projection.

Preparation.

You have to prepare yourself properly before you can successfully astral project. It takes a long, long time of hard work and practice before you can just sit down and pop out. Only the best and most dedicated lightworkers and healers may achieve this status. Us mere mortals have to gradually glide into the process and gently persuade our bodies to let go of part of its consciousness and astral body. Here are some important points:

Learn the meditation properly by heart. This is easier than you think. You cannot project while you're reading this text. Get into a steady life-rhythm. Wake up at the same time; go to bed at the same time. The body really appreciates this! Try to get as much good sleep as you can. 8 hours a night is the absolute minimum. 10 hours is much better. Get plenty of physical exercise. This will release energy blocks and thus allow energy to flow more vigorously through your body. Watch your diet! Try to stay away from arousing stuff as much as possible. No hot or spicy foods stay low on fat. No coffee or chocolate (try herbal tea instead) and

ABSOLUTELY NO ALCOHOL! Trying to project while under the influence of this drug can get you into SERIOUS TROUBLE. Try to eat no meat, or, if this is hard for you, as little as you can. Try drinking plenty of water (no mineral water). A big mug of water with some freshly squeezed lemon juice can be a great coffee substitute at breakfast. Pick a regular time at which you may try to project. This can be at night, in the afternoon or in the morning. Just make it the same time every time. The body doesn't like surprises, a good general rule. Before you try to astral project, concentrate on it. This may start hours, days or even weeks in advance. Persuade yourself that you ARE going to achieve it someday, and visualise yourself being out of the body already. This gets your being in the right frame of mind. Make sure you will NOT be disturbed while you perform the meditation.

Disconnect the phone; any disturbance to this meditation (or any meditation) can be extremely annoying and off-putting. Pay attention to other disturbing factors, your clothes for example, your clothes may be too tight, so make sure that you wear something loose and comfortable Room temperature is another factor, not too cold, not too warm. Disconnect all the electrical wiring that surrounds you. They can generate disturbing energy fields. In fact, any steel/iron/metal in and on your body can seriously interfere with your energy-flows.

So take out those earrings and tongue piercing. Any acupuncturist can tell you that it's not a good idea to just jam a piece of metal in your nervous system. If you insist on using music through the meditation, that's fine. It doesn't work for me, though. I always end up just listening to the music instead. Make your room very dimly lit. This will relax your eyes, a very important and often neglected step. Getting out is very difficult when your eyes are still hard at work.

If you feel you're not up to it, then don't do it. You will most likely not be able to project and this will only lead to disappointment and eventually break your morale. Always remember that it's a natural process and that you can and will do it. A few hours before the meditation, open all the windows and doors in your room and allow fresh air to blow through it. You may want to use incense burn it beforehand and then extinguish the fire. Your body will instinctively react to fire burning somewhere in your room and relaxing will become very difficult. Make sure all your body's needs are satisfied, so remember to go to the bathroom before you start your meditation. Make sure you're not hungry, nor thirsty. Don't eat anything 'heavy' before meditating.

Lie down, with your head pointing to the East. Relax. Make sure you're in a comfortable position. Make sure your spine and neck are quite straight. You may need a pillow to support your head. Breathe rhythmically in and out very deeply. Concentrate on your breath. Feel it flowing through your body, down, through your lungs, cooling your ribs, all the way down to your belly breathe like a baby. Do this until you have reached a very relaxed posture and breathing rhythm. This may take a while, so don't rush things. Now do muscle relaxations exercise? Clench your toes for a few seconds, and then relax. Feel the fatigue taking over your muscles. Do this again.

Do the same with all your muscles, working from bottom to top, your legs, your bottom, your belly, your chest, your hands and arms, your neck etc. Particularly important is relaxing your face!

Try to really wear out your facial muscles. Stick out your tongue as far as you can, make funny faces, clench your jaw, lift your head a little of the floor, make yourself look like an idiot (this is why there should be no other people present :). Then feel the fatigue and warm relaxation take over. Also try to relax your eyes this way. Now comes the main meditation. It is made up out of four parts:

1. Energizing
2. Protection
3. Formulating the Astral Vehicle
4. Actual Projection

1. The energizing meditation is actually a very good meditation to perform whenever you feel like it. It balances out your chakras and makes you feel fit and clear. It's also very important to perform this meditation after having (whether or not successfully) tried to astral project, because it will rebalance your being again.

On an out' breath, visualize the Crown centre (the top of your head) as a sphere of brilliant, white light. Keep on breathing until you get a steady image. On an in' breath, draw down a shaft of white light to your next centre, in this case the Brow (your forehead, the third eye between your eyebrows). On an out' breath, visualize a sphere of dove-grey light on your forehead. Make sure you get a steady image. On an in' breath, draw down a shaft of white light from your forehead to your throat etc. Here are all the centres and their colours. The shaft is always made of white light. Visualize the spheres as being part inside and part outside your body. When you visualize a sphere, quickly recap all the spheres you already 'energized'.

Top of Head - Brilliant white
Forehead - Dove-grey
Throat - Intense mid-purple
Heart - Radiant Yellow
Genitals - Lavender, radiant and swirling
Earth (under your feet) - The seven prismatic colours (rainbow) swirling lazily.

Once you have energized your whole body like this, concentrate on all the spheres and shafts at once. Be aware of all the colours. After having done this exercises a number of times, you will feel tingling in the centres when you energize them. You will feel your solar plexus (in the middle of your body, right between your belly button and ribs) throbbing like crazy. Here's where you will come to know astral substance. Hold the spheres for a few more seconds, and then let them slowly fade away.

2. The protection. Visualize a large sphere of radiant white light lying at your feet, until you get a steady image. Breathe in, and pull all that light in a long white shaft up through your body to the top of your head.

See it light up the inside of your body, leaving a steady shine. On an out breath, let the light flow down along the outside of your body, encapsulating you in a waterfall of white, protective light. Let the light recollect at your feet and at an in-breath, pull it back up again. This is a greatly relaxing exercise, and it makes you feel great. Repeat this cycle for as long as you like, at least 10 times.

3. Now you have to formulate your astral vehicle i.e.; the 'car' your conscious/spirit needs to 'travel' in. Here's how to do it. Visualize a jet of blue-silver mist to leave your body at your solar plexus. Make it form a cloud a few feet above you. Then form this cloud into a human figure, floating above you, facing down towards you. This human figure decides what you're going to look like in the Astral plane, but don't worry! You can remodel this figure in great detail once you're out there. It is a good idea however, to, prior to the meditation, concentrate on how you want to look like.

Once you're happy with this visualization, stop the flow of astral substance, but keep the fine line between you and the vehicle intact.

IMPORTANT: if you don't succeed in projecting, ALWAYS make an effort to 'take back' the exteriorised i.e. astral substance. Make the figure into a cloud again, and pull it back. This will prevent unnecessary and severe energy loss and fatigue.

4. The actual projection. Pick a point on your body. Any point will do. The solar plexus is probably the best because it's right where your astral vehicle is attached to your body. The third eye point is another excellent point, because it's your connection to your soul. Now, collect your being, yourself, everything you are, all your wishes, thoughts, and movements into this point.
Its like crawling away into a grain of sand. Empty your head, your legs, arms etc. and recollect yourself at this specific point.

Now visualize the same point on your astral vehicle, that's still floating above you.
Now, make a mental resolution to lift this point where you are out of your body, along the line (cord) that links you with your vehicle, into your vehicle, to the same point in your vehicle, and SEE IT HAPPEN. Now the hard part: make a mental effort to 'turn around' in your astral vehicle thus come to face your own body lying a few feet away. Now expand your personality again, and make it fill your astral vehicle. This is rather like putting on a thick glove.

Make yourself aware of your new body. You've done it! You can fly! Wee! Have a good time!

Important notes:
- The first time it actually happens, don't do much more than just floating in air and looking at your body. Keep this up as long as you can, then slowly 'drift down'. You will automatically 'snap back' (this is very much like what can happen to you when you're lying in bed, when you get that feeling like you're falling down.

I have already said that we all astral project while we're sleeping).This 'snapping back' will happen more often than you wish for the first few times you achieved actual projection. Don't worry. You have learned the 'knack' and there's no reason why you cannot do it again. You will learn how to stay out there for a longer period of time automatically. Once you're out there comfortably, and you're ready to explore, get away from your body as quickly as possible, because, even looking at your body, or getting close, may cause you to be snapped back.

Greetings

Closure

A Final Word

I have already mentioned in my introduction, that the subtle body thrives a lot on subdued light, energy, subdued time quite time or something like your meditation i.e. the crystallite body. There are people on the planet earth at present who have made this shift (crystallite body) in fact there are 500 at present living on light as they call it or DOW Divine light within.

www.selfempowermenacademy.com

So with our new hospital in China and people living on light or Prana in many parts of the world, maybe this book is not as far out of reach as it seemed when reading the first few chapters

Though in saying that, some perhaps after reading this book may find it hard to visualise a world of the seven vibrations a world where illness never appeared physically at all. Well the world would certainly be a different world than the one we live in now. This would be a very large paradigm change perhaps even a quantum leap. (Quantum leaps are places where the paradigm is shifted more than usual). Western medical and drug companies would be put out of business! In fact, everything that western medicine now stands for would be obsolete and considered a primitive understanding of human health and healing. If simply addressing the mental or emotional attitudes or environmental stressors that disturb the human aura could treat cancer, then medicine would most certainly be a science of emotional and mental readjusting. Yes, paradigms do fight change—especially profitable economical ones! New kinds of healers would appear in society, healers that would not only fully understand the physical body, but would also understand and study the Chakras and auric layers. They would study the "organs" of the human aura, learning its psychological and emotional functions, and how to affect healing in the auric level. Doctors would use electric or magnetic instruments such as light or sound, thought or emotional power, or other means as yet undiscovered. There would be college courses, economical home courses for the studying and understanding of the Chakra and auric level, which would be just as essential as anatomy courses.

This would become the merging of western medicine and what is now called metaphysical healing.

Imagine what it would be like if every second and third level student had full knowledge of how the human aura and its centre (or organs) work? Could people be taught to avoid all the pitfalls of the past generations physical and emotional disorders which perhaps happen to some extent or another by not addressing and understanding the Chakra and aura system of the human body? Could human beings be born enlightened and stay enlightened, not just sinking into negative patterns of unawareness and fear? And what is there after enlightenment, to the mass conscious entity we called humanity? How would a human world be changed without the conflict of physical illness in high quantities like it is today, with huge business profits built around it? People would actually be able to heal themselves and not need the services of a doctor...ever.

In today's world, humans operate out of a state of fear (or root Chakra blockages) even if it is unconscious fear or what is called "low level" fear.

The main fear for almost every human on Earth is fear for personal physical survival. The drive underneath almost every activity is somehow connected with physical survival, even the craving for love from others, workaholics striving for financial security, and various other effortful endeavours. Every human is trying to avoid sickness, poverty, and death. Even people who have plenty have feelings of being a have-not because they are striving to collect enough savings to alleviate the fear of poverty, which could result in survival issues. And let us not forget the people who are actually in a life and death situation on a daily basis, with many in a constant fear of losing all. There is a basic belief across the mass consciousness of humanity that there is "not enough" for everyone and humans believe there must be a struggle to survive. So people do jobs they hate to serve this need. People go through all sorts of physical healing, keeping fit, losing weight, etc, to preserve life for even just another year, truly neglecting the spirit. There is a prevailing struggle for survival across the globe that is reflected in everything, from global struggles for survival to the struggles between individuals.

What would happen if physical and etheric medicine merged, resulting in a world without physical disorders, and what are the spiritual implications? The spiritual implications for humans exploring the auric layers will be immense. Humans still struggle greatly with little or no awareness of the functioning of their physical, emotional or mental bodies, unaware of patterns that must be broken for true health to emerge. The starting point in life for our children or grandchildren would be in the heart i.e. in spiritual evolution, rather than the physical survival level, as it is now. The next era for humanity's evolution might well be the heart. Humanity is mastering the physical, emotional and mental levels of existence, and then comes the heart, the fourth layer of the human aura or the fourth Chakra i.e. the bridge between the higher and lower centres and layers. This is when the exploration of the higher levels of human existence will begin. New kinds of adventures await humanity in the higher levels of existence i.e. the seven vibrations that the Chakras and auric layers represent as a connection to these realities? I believe there would be new kinds of energies invented, new kinds of social structures, new kinds of science, especially spiritual sciences, like astral travel, time travel, telekinesis, manipulating matter with sound, tele-transportation, and inter-dimensional travel. Physical laws could possibly be bent once the deeper levels of reality are understood, and the higher (or deeper) aspects of humankind's existence are embraced.

In the seventh vibration which is the quantum leap talked about in this book, other dimensions and universes are huge. Humans have only begun to explore them through meditation. Perhaps using fossil fuels and projecting our physical bodies into space is the wrong approach for travel in the cosmos! I personally believe that the direction for travel in the universe is an inward journey, not a physical one. Consciousness is faster than light. Perhaps the universe is a virtual reality already built into our system as humans, at least seven layers of virtual reality, and we only have to move inward to experience them. Perhaps the astral body is better equipped for space travel than the physical body. The ability to enter the other worlds, in which the human exists parallel to his or her physical existence, is a by-product of meditation, awakening the Chakras and harmonizing the auric field. This does not necessarily mean that there must be full consciousness of the Chakras and auras, for meditation will adjust these automatically, but quieting the mind is the first step to attaining the ability to reach these other worlds, that the human being might simultaneously exist in, with a more expanded "mind."

The human energy field is the next frontier for western medicine to explore. When doctors and scientists understand it completely, illness will be a thing of the past. There has been enough scientific research and enough proof that the human aura is real and is not just a product of fantasy as some would like to believe. The human energy field not only shows illness before it appears at the physical level, but it is also easily influenced, especially by the mind of the person who owns the aura. There are countless researchers who have documented and studied the human aura and its properties i.e. Kirlians discoveries. After seeing the proof of scientific research on the study of the human auric field, who could possibly doubt the reality of its existence? Today the study continues in numerous technologies i.e. Instrumental Tran Communication or ITC for short which is a range of technologies and means by which communications arriving from the Astral worlds can be received and stored by technical equipment such as tape recorders, TV's, radios, computers, telephones, mini- disk recorders, video recorders, and many other devices already being used or that will be used in the future in order to obtain these contacts from the Astral Worlds.

Indeed ever since the discovery of the electric light in the 1920's by Thomas Edison, one of the greatest scientist of our time, ITC is rapidly evolving and will continue to do so in the future. Indeed ITC in the future will be the bridge between a third dimension time frame and a seventh vibration multidimensional time frame. In 2001 Mark Macy a leading researcher in ITC for many years was experiencing"miracles "in his laboratory i.e. colour images of spirits and loud clear dialogue on a reliable basis. So now as we come to the end of this book which may perhaps be quite hard to swallow yet, but hopefully through the advances of ITC scientist and researchers like Mark Macy; can prove to Mankind in more compelling ways the survival of the spirit than perhaps traditional channelling often viewed with cynicism and scepticism then this book has done it's job and will be not regarded as being a paranormal fantasy. Perhaps one day the paranormal will be regarded as being normal as we make the next quantum leap to the seventh vibration as people generally have more faith in scientific evidence, which is more physically tangible than traditional channelling. So it is clear now more that ever that we need science to make the shift to the seven vibration but it is also very clear that scientists themselves need to take this quantum leap to the seventh vibration and to follow in the footsteps of the geniuses of Einstein and Bonham and the likes who have paved the way for the next step of human evolution.

Indeed it is clear that the field of ITC is proving to be very important in proving the continuity of life after death of the physical body and of the inner realities i.e. Arturus, Sirius and Pleiades, etc. The works of the people like Mark Macy and the world ITC, together with numerous scientists, researchers and of course **you** / lightworkers who have made the shift to the seventh vibration and whose time and efforts will become progressively more important as one of mans routes to inner level of Spirit communication and enlightenment.

Conclusion

So enlightenment and healing is at hand, and is within our reach. Humanity has become more fascinated with the ideas around meditation and its healing properties than ever before. Coming into the heart layer of the aura, which allows for the experiences of enlightenment to begin, is a result of mastering the physical, emotional and mental layers of the human aura. Over the past few decades alone, leaps and bounds have been made in the fields of metaphysical, of knowledge of the physical emotional and mental layers of the human aura body and healing properties.

It is not that this knowledge does not exist, but rather, that it is being largely ignored and unused by the majority. The ability to love, to have compassion, and to be merciful are qualities human beings on a mass level are still attempting to create in themselves. Compassion is a new idea, and it is the bridge, the password, to the higher (deeper) levels of human experience. Those who have the ability to have unconditional love, or at least compassion and acceptance of the human condition in others are able to make this quantum leap and move to the next levels of experience, what many people call enlightenment or what is called in this book the seventh vibration. With those levels of harmony in every person, physical illness in the masses would be impossible. So let us use the knowledge that we have already gathered about the physical, emotional and mental layers of the human aura, the first three, and explore them fully. Let us truly reap the benefits of such explorations. It is the first three layers of each individual that must be healed before humanity will stop its struggle within itself. A world of physical health and well-being is within our grasp if we unlock the mysteries of the aura with research and study. Let us learn the laws of the human aura, for it does obey laws of some sort in each layer. Let us perform the balancing needed for healing on all three levels, physical, emotional, and mental, and see what happens next. This would be a great place to start.

Greetings

Finally

When I sat down to write this book I had no thoughts in my mind what I was going to write about apart from the name of the book and the name of the chambers and of course the word Greetings.

All throughout this book, which I personally believe, is channelled through me by a higher intelligence and which describes a world within a world, described, as been the seventh vibration. Looking at the chapters and introduction this does seem like a magical world, a place where one would like to be. Although this book states that imagination is the greatest gift of all and for all times, however, this book also states that we should not let our imagination run amuck and keep things practical, down to earth and in the right perspective. The book tells us that we should not use our imagination to escape into a fairytale world away from this world or it's responsibilities, but to use our imagination to create our own reality and to explore the inner realms. However in saying this, one may still query here, "is this for real "or "is this nothing more that the product of my imagination" or perhaps "nothing more that the outcome of my distorted mind?". However it will be agreed by most thinkers that there is communication between worlds of many different dimensions and that we're all connected. Anyone who thinks otherwise is welcome to do so.

The power to connect for mankind is indeed within the abilities of each and every one of us and always has been. It is not about spending all of our time and wealth on space exploration or building up huge arsenals of arms as a super power in a world beyond a temporal illusion of space and time. The power to connect is not at all to be found in a 3-D illusionary universe but it is to be found within the inner spheres of reality beyond the temporal illusion of space and time. One can indeed explore the real universe by astral and mental projection and other natural abilities; this is the future. In the future everyone without exception; governments, church leaders etc will become more aware of a multi dimension time frame of the seven vibrations and will give willingly of their time and wealth to those that need it most.

To conclude:

When you come to realise that life, your life and the other lives you lived, is a connection with many other souls of a game being played on this stage we call earth in the drama of life itself you will then look at yourself with new awareness breaking away from the old consciousness that you have felt trapped in for so long over many life times, You will then realize that there is no separation from me to you, or from them to us, we are all connected; this is the power to connect.

Finally I leave you, with these words of inspiration

"To my beloved ones the universal beings of love and light embrace you all this day. We offer you the seven magical energies of time immorally. Every single one of you is emerging in the Christ like energy. Hold true to you mission, how humble it may appear to be, speak the truth, spread the light, live your life with honour and passion, without fear of judgement and don't let density stand in your way of being your ultimate self. For if you're aware of it or not, you are moving into the higher vibration of light, achieving self Mastery and ascension in this lifetime, believe it "it is possible."

Greetings

About the Author

Charles Shovlin hails from the townland of Kilraine outside Glenties, Co. Donegal Ireland.

From a small farming background he received his national and secondary education locally and still lives in Kilraine with his wife Grace and their three sons Hugh, Peter and Daniel.

Charles is one of the founding pioneers of Tai Chi in Ireland and is one of the first Irishmen to publish a book on the subject.

He has also produced and distributed his own Tai Chi video. He has taught and given many lectures and workshops on Tai Chi and healing and in 2006 he published his autobiography "The Journey Home", and in 2007 he published "A way To Healing The Seven Set Practice"

He is a renowned healer and people travel from all over Donegal and beyond to his Castle Healing Centre in Kilraine. He has been featured regularly in both local and Scottish radio and printed media over a number of years, and has appeared on R.T.E.'s Nationwide television programme in Feb 2002.

"The Power To Connect". This book which Charles personal ly believes is channelled through him by a higher intelligence and which describes a world within a world, described, as being the Seventh Vibration.

This is Charles' fourth book; it is another inspirational read with loads of inspiring messages filled with hope and love, which is most inspiring at this particular time when the world is gripped in fear and confusion.

This book will expand your mind and reconnect you to a higher intelligence of collective consciousness within yourself; i.e. your soul

Remember what you choose to believe or what you choose not to believe within these writings for whatever reason; is not important, but what is important is that you connect to the true spirit within, as there is no separation from me to you or from them to us.

The Castle Taiji Healing Centre in Kilraine

Yes after almost 20 years Charles continues to give relief, to the sick, lonely and broken spirits who continue to come to his Castle Healing Centre or as some would say to the most unusual turf shed in Donegal.

Charles continues to guide people who come to him for his expert advice, teaching, healing and on the gentle arts of tai chi and qi-gong and energy related topics. He is a renowned healer and people travel from all over Donegal and beyond to his Castle Healing Centre in Kilraine. He has been featured regularly in both local & Scottish radio and printed media over a number of years, and has appeared on R.T.E.'s nationwide television programme in Feb 2002.

Other works by Charles J. Shovlin

Books

Tai Chi For Everyone

This book describes the postures, mainly taken from the Yang Cheng- Fu form of Taiji both moving and static with the help of photographs and diagrams, and explains the health benefits that go with each posture. The author has made every effort to describe the exercises in as simple a way as possible. If you are a novice you should find the video/DVD "Tai Chi For Everyone" a useful accompaniment to the book.

isbn 0-9545-7800-7

Order on line www.lulu.com

The Journey Home

This book tells the story of the Castle and explained how the Castle Taiji Healing Centre was born. The centre which now allows him to see hundreds of clients on a regular basis, with the hope of bringing them some peace of mind, so that they to will find their niche - their own "journey home".

isbn 1-4120-6602-6

Order on line www. Amazon .com

Order on line www.Trafford.com/05-1513

A Way To Healing The Seven Set Practice

This book; is purely inspirational and deals with healing in a truly open minded way. It is written to take the myth out of healing and to stop it from been labelled. This book clearly states that healing has no boundaries, only those we put on it ourselves.

isbn 1-906018-14-6

Order on line www.amazon .com

Order on line www.originalwriting.ie/bookshop

VIDEOS & DVD

Tai-Chi For Everyone & The Seven Set Practice

Tel 074 -95 -51596